# A Sign from Heaven

# A Sign from Heaven

## The possible Last message from God to The 21$^{st}$ Century

### Nancy A. McGill

I have changed the names of the identifying characters of the other two people in this true story to honor their privacy. Everyone else in this story is real, including me. Excerpts- taken from Fatima for Today. Pages 249-261 Permission given by Ignatius Press

Front cover and book design by A. Gemmail.

Back cover and book design by Fr. Gordon Macray.

Available at Shakespeare & Co.

939 Lexington Avenue, NYC

212-772-3400

ISBN: 978-0-9986651-8-4

Library of Congress Control Number: 2015902008

LCCN Imprint Name: New York, NY

# Table of Contents

## *Special Dedication*

I wish to dedicate this book to the most holy Queen of Heaven for coming back to earth again as she promised she would to sister Lucia, at Fatima.

The Queen of heaven kept her promise, only this time "She" came with the angels to New York City-America, to bring the message from God straight to the heart of power.

I thank my parents for raising me and introducing me to the Catholic/Christian faith that became a solid foundation in my life and kept me on the straight and narrow and for teaching me to know and love Our Lady.

# *Foreword*

I have known Nancy for a few years through an early editing and organizing process for this book. She is an emotionally honest person. I am so glad that she is now presenting her work for us all to read!

Nancy's story is of amazing events in 1993, of other spiritual events early in life, and her personal reactions to all of it. She describes the events of an evening when she and two friends encountered a beautiful angel, and Our Lady, the Blessed Mother who was sharing an urgent message for the world. Nancy candidly shares her fears and feelings, conveying the importance of it all. She tells of her reaching out to the clergy, going from priest to priest, some supporting and some hesitating. She tells how the Church where the event occurred was built, and mixes in some important but not usually heard social history.

Her voice is innocent and candid, vacillating between nonfiction episodes and opinion pieces that would sound well from the pulpit or a soap box. She intersperses her writing with poignant poetic quotations, betraying a gift for the metaphor, my favorite explainer.

Nancy describes her trials and tribulations and devotion, and they compare to the Blessed Mother's. She has a premonition of 9/11, fate seems to direct her labor to the survivors at the site, and she notes connections between the two awesome events. She wrestles with some emotional scars, and with her friends' fear to stand with her. She tells us of her private dreams, so perhaps we can make our own sense of her magnificent story.

Her book is a call to caring about our world, a warning of things to come, and she makes a bold well deserved move to opining on recent current events. We all feel the threat of terrorism, and live with it. Nancy speaks to, with, and of that fear with, at times, the tone of a fiery sermon.

Devoted Mary followers will enjoy the author's narration of the events that happened to her and with other Mary sightings, and what happened as she pondered her next actions and pursued her questions.

SEAN MAHONY, JANUARY 15

LOURDE—LA VIERGE DE LA GROTTE

## THE HAIL MARY

HAIL MARY, full of grace.

The Lord is with thee. Blessed art thou among women,

And blessed is the fruit of thy womb, Jesus.

Holy Mary, mother of God,

Pray for us sinners, now

and at the hour of our death.

    Amen.

# *Preface*

Even though I've always felt a presence around me, I thought it was there for everyone. It was not until my grandma passed on that I began to take more notice of my invisible friends, and I realized that I was more in tune with another angelic life-force from somewhere else, which I presumed was Heaven. From a very early age, I have shared my life with angels and the holy spirits. I have been blessed with the gift of being able to see the invisible; God became a very important part of my life and always will be.

I have lived by this philosophy. My faith in God comes first above all else—before my faith in man. What I see (and have seen since I was a child) is not, and was not, childish imaginations in my mind. This is real; it's another part of life that does indeed exist in another dimension. The angels and holy spirits are my friends. The story that I am about to tell you is a true story—it's the real deal, it really happened, and no one should discount it, because it concerns the world.

# Introduction

This is not an ordinary book—in fact, it's an extraordinary book. Simply put, it's about the supernatural world and the natural world. Each world is on its own plane, but they both have the capacity to very gently collide with one another. This can happen when the natural world is in trouble. For example, when human actions threaten our world to the point of total destruction and annihilation, and there seems to be no hope for a way out, signals are then sent up to the supernatural world in the form of prayers, novenas, recitations of the holy rosary to the Blessed Mother, sacrifices, and true repentance for our sins.

The supernatural or spiritual world—also known as Heaven—hears humankind's pleas for help, and because God is good, merciful, and forgiving, He will never refuse His children, provided that they are sincere and do penance. It's a simple philosophy—love, honor, and obey God. Because people cannot survive on their own in this world, they need God the Father, the Son, and the Holy Ghost. People can never be happy in the natural and physical world because the supernatural, spiritual world is their true home. Through prayers, you can invite the supernatural into your world. It will never intrude unless invited.

Jesus occasionally sends His beloved Mother, whom we know as the Blessed Mother. She loves us so much; she wants souls to go to Heaven so that we may be close to Jesus. But she can only do so much to help us save our souls—we have to help ourselves, and that starts from within. Our faith gives us the strength to go through the trials and hardships in our lives. It is our faith that will lead us to God and through the narrow gate that leads to Heaven.

God does exist, and from time to time, He sends visions and apparitions of the Blessed Virgin Mary and angels specifically to let us unfortunate mortals down here in the physical, natural world know that we are definitely not alone; the angels will lovingly guide us on our journey and pilgrimage to the other world.

As there are natural laws of the physical world, there are also natural laws of the supernatural world, and it is in our best interests to obey the laws of God. If we acknowledge Him and His laws, I'm sure we will be on the right track. As for me, the last thing I want to do is offend God.

This great universe, which we see by day and by night and call the natural world, is ruled by fixed laws that the Creator has imposed upon it, and those wonderful laws secure us against any substantial injury or loss. One portion of the natural world might conflict with another, and there might be changes in it internally, but viewed as a whole, it is adapted to stand forever. Hence the psalmist says, "He has established the world which shall not be moved" (Card, 1955 p. 136).

Such is the world of nature; but there is another and still more wonderful world. There is a power that avails to alter and subdue this visible world and to suspend and counteract its laws; that is, the world of angels and saints, of the holy Church and her children. The weapon by which they master its laws is the power of prayer.

## OUR FATHER

Our Father who is in Heaven,

hallowed be your name

thy kingdom come,

thy will be done on earth,

as it is in heaven,

give us this day our daily bread

as we forgive those who trespass against us

and lead us not into temptation

but deliver us from evil.

Amen

# Part 1

## Early Recollections and Encounters with the Supernatural World

*My awareness of the supernatural world began when I was a* baby. I remember that when I heard the name Jesus mentioned at home, I would get excited; I did not want to go to bed because I wanted to hear more about Him. Whenever I heard His name, I listened eagerly to the story that the speaker was telling. It held my interest. To me, Jesus was like a special member of the family who was away somewhere and would come home one day.

The following vignettes are my recollections of my encounters with the supernatural world from childhood and into adulthood.

# Chapter 1

## Gran Visits Her Friend— My First Vision

*I remember one day when I was about four years old, my* beloved Gran took me with her to visit her friend. Clutching my doll with one hand and hanging on to Gran with the other, I crossed the street with Gran and climbed the rickety old front stairs that were almost white with years of scrubbing, a weekly ritual that was practiced by the housewives in Glasgow back then.

As we reached the top of the fourteen stairs of the brownstone, Gran knocked on the door. A teary-eyed woman opened the door and led us into her kitchen. She showed Gran the oven while talking about her daughter who had fallen onto the floor and had cut her forehead above the right eye; the woman demonstrated this by pointing to her forehead. While they were talking, I wandered into another room and saw a light brown casket containing a pretty, young girl about seventeen years old.

She had long brown hair and was wearing a white shroud. She was sitting up in the casket and was talking to someone at the other end of the room as if she were explaining what had happened to her.

I looked over toward the other part of the room, but I could not see whom she was talking to. I did see the gash on her forehead above her right eye. It did not seem to bother her that she was dead.

Apparently, the girl was not aware of my presence in the room. Coming from a country where children were seen and not heard, especially back then, and being very shy, I kept it to myself, but I have never forgotten the experience. I was not afraid of the dead girl because I was so young and really did not understand the concept of death.

# Chapter 2

# A Message from an Angel

*Not long after my Gran passed away, I was missing her terribly* because I had been so close to her. One Sunday morning after Mass, Uncle Tommy and I were at my grandparents' grave. He was busy fixing the grave and arranging the flowers when suddenly I received a message; it was my very first message or communication from the supernatural world. I whispered to Uncle Tommy that I had just received a message.

He looked around to see if anyone was near us and said, "What are you talking about, and what kind of message? What did it say?"

I said, "Someone told me that everything that will happen on the earth, world events, would all happen in my time."

He asked me if I saw anything or anyone.

"No, I did not see anyone, but I did hear it, in a divine wind."

Uncle Tommy's reaction was matter-of-fact, and he remarked that it must have been an angel, and then he went back to arranging the flowers. We knelt down and prayed.

Where had this message come from? It was strange, indeed. At that time, I knew nothing of the world; I was sheltered by my family. The only world I knew was my immediate family, the neighbors, my little friends, and the chapel and priests. Looking back, I know it was an angel sent from Heaven that had come to give me the message about the future of the world.

"The wind blows where it chooses, and you hear the sound of it, but you know not where it comes from or where it goes. So it is with everyone who is born of the Spirit" (John 3:8).

# Chapter 3

## My Friend in the Sky

*I recall a summer's day a couple of years later when I was* between six and seven years old, not long after my Gran had died. I was at home with my big sister, Mary (the family called her May for short). She was babysitting me and let me go outside to play by myself. I could not have been out very long, perhaps about fifteen minutes, when suddenly I had a very strange experience. My attention was drawn up toward the sky. I looked up and found myself face-to-face with a young man. He was very high up in the sky. I remember stepping back a bit and crossing my hands over my heart because I was very young and afraid. But there was no need to be afraid, and he was incredibly beautiful. The vision seemed to be toward the left side of my eyesight, directly across from the old church, which was about a stone's throw from my parents' house at 83 Dale Street, Glasgow, Scotland. It all happened so quickly. Although he was very far away and high up in the sky, at the same time, we had direct eye-to-eye contact. The only way I can explain it is like this: it's as though I had been looking through a zoom lens, which seemed to cut the distance between us and enabled me to have direct eye contact with my newfound friend from the sky. Time and distance seemed to disappear. In other words, the vision seemed to amplify or project itself to bring itself closer to me, perhaps to help me understand that we are not alone in this world.

I was fully focused on him. This beautiful young man was about in his early thirties, although at that time it was hard for me to tell his age. But I do know that he was the most beautiful person I had ever seen and had beautiful blue eyes, bluer than the sky. He had light-brown hair that was parted in the middle and was almost shoulder length. He had a neat, fine-pointed beard that was the same color as his hair. He was wearing a creamy-white robe draped with a pale-red sash across his right side. His arms were outstretched. He seemed very sad, and I immediately had the impression that he felt sorry for me. Although he did not speak to me verbally, he did communicate to me through mental telepathy. I picked up his message, and he was telling me that I was going to have a hard life followed by suffering. Young as I was, I knew that something major would happen to me at some point in my life—and also to the world.

He looked sad that the stage had been set and nothing would—could—change.

It's strange, but I remember that day feeling that we were related in some way, because he certainly knew me better than I knew him. He was full of compassion for me; he was definitely from another dimension: "the holy other." Some things of that day I wish to keep to myself.

I ran into the house to fetch my big sister May, and I called out to her, "I have seen a man in the sky." I pulled her outside to show her, and I pointed toward the sky. "He was up there. Can you see him?"

"No, I can't see anything," she said, searching the sky.

My poor sister strained her eyes looking; the man must have gone back to Heaven. By now, the vision had gone. However, I did notice that a large part of the sky where the vision had been was now a very bright red.

Of course, my sister told my parents about it when they came home. We were a quiet and close-knit family. I do not think my father made much of it; to him, I was just a child, and back then, children were seen and not heard. My parents told the priest about my experience, and that was that. Everybody forgot about it, except me. I cried and pined every day for my friend in the sky to come back to me, but he never did come back. I couldn't understand why this person from another world could mean much more to me than my own family. It was beyond my understanding. He played a major part in my life. I thought about him all the time and I was heartbroken that he never came back. I drove my poor father crazy by asking him a million questions, and it always ended with the same one: "Dad, will he ever come back? I need to see him again."

Dad always consoled me. "You need to have patience. Yes, maybe one day, he will come back; just keep going to Mass and saying your prayers." This continued until I was into my twenties.

A couple of my friends would ask me from time to time, "Have you ever seen your vision again?"

Sadly, I would always give them the same answer: "No."

They would try to reassure me by saying, "Well, maybe one day he will come back; perhaps it will happen midway through your life."

I grew to love him and will always love my beautiful friend in the sky.

I carried on with my life, resigned to the fact that I might never see him again, and tried to let go, but that was impossible for me to do, as I have said before. He is a major part of my life that I cannot abandon. Many people have come and gone in my life, but my friend in the sky always has that special place in my heart. In a spiritual sense, he really was my first true friend outside of my family.

Later on, my family told me that my friend from the sky was "the Sacred Heart of Jesus." I do admit that my vision did indeed look like the Sacred Heart of Jesus, only at that time back then, I did not know Jesus because I was too young. One day, my Aunt Rose showed me a picture of the Sacred Heart of Jesus. Yes, it was close to what I had seen on that day.

I remember one day in class the teacher was talking about Jesus, and she held up a large picture of Jesus to show the class. I thought to myself, "He does not look like my Jesus."

But one thing I do know for sure is that very special day changed the course of my life, and the image of him was imprinted on my brain forever.

## Prayer

"Come, Holy Spirit, enkindle within us the fire of your love. Teach us to abide in the heart of Jesus that we may learn the secret of all secrets, the truth of all truths: God is love.

To fall in love with God is the greatest of all romances;
to seek Him, the greatest adventure;
to find Him, the greatest human achievement."

—St. Augustine

# Sacred Heart

Merciful Jesus, I consecrate
myself today and always to
Your Most Sacred Heart.
Most Sacred Heart of Jesus
I implore, that I may ever
love You more and more.
Most Sacred Heart of Jesus
I trust in You !
Most Sacred Heart of Jesus
have mercy on us !
Most Sacred Heart of Jesus
I believe in Your love for me.
Jesus, meek and humble of
heart, make my heart like
Your Heart.

*Photo: Claude Alliez.*

# Chapter 4

## Dale Street

*Dale Street, where I grew up in Glasgow, Scotland, is only a* small street, but so many things happened on that street. My first pet and best friend was Prince, a beautiful black-and-white-spotted Dalmatian. I loved him so much. One night just after dinner, I heard him whimpering. I rushed out to find him. He had been hit by a car, and he hobbled into the hallway to find me. I cradled him in my arms; I sang an old Irish lullaby as Prince died in my arms. Eventually, my father moved from Dale Street, and it broke my heart; I wanted to stay near that spot. Part of me still remains there on Dale Street where it all began.

Thinking back, something very traumatic and devastating did happen there just off Dale Street on the main road even before my spiritual experience of Jesus. I had a little friend, and her name was Ann Taylor. Her parents would bring her into Glasgow for the weekends. We would play together, and sometimes we would sit on the steps of my grandparents' house. We would stare at the moon and wonder what it was, where it came from, and why it was just sitting up there all by itself.

My friend Ann would say to me, "Do you think it is lonely?"

I would reply, "I do not know; maybe we should wave to it." And that's what we would do: we would wave and blow kisses to the moon.

Then one late afternoon, Ann was crossing the main street that intersects with Dale Street to get ice cream when she was hit by a double-decker bus and killed instantly. I knew that my little friend was under the large bus. I crouched down at the side of the bus, and I could see her lying on her side as if she were asleep. She was still wearing her little tartan-plaid pixie hat that she always wore. From that day on, I prayed for my little friend every day and still include her in my prayers. I am sure Ann is in Heaven, and there is an extra star that shines ever so brightly near the moon.

Like flowers along a fragrant path are the friends God gives along Life's way. Every path He guides us on is fragrant with His loving –kindness

Psalm 25:10 TLB

## PRAYER FOR FRIENDS
(An Old French Prayer)

Blessed Mother of those whose
names you can read in my heart, watch
over them with every care. Make their
way easy and their labors fruitful. Dry
their tears if they weep; sanctify their
joys; raise their  courage if they weaken;
restore their hope if they lose heart,
their health if they be ill, truth  if they
err, and repentance if they fall.

Amen.

# Chapter 5

## Solitude in Church

*Many times, I would have the impulse to go to the chapel and* pray, regardless of the weather.

My mother would ask me, "Where on earth are you going? It's a blizzard out; it's not fit for man or beast."

I'd say, "Mom, it's important; I want to go the chapel."

Sometimes, there was a sense of urgency, and at the same time, it was a warm and beautiful feeling. I would go to the chapel because there, in the quietness and the holiness, I could get in touch with my soul to reflect and examine my conscience and clear my head so that I could pray sincerely to God. I took great consolation in knowing that God saw everything.

I would also pray to Jesus and Our Lady, whom I had adopted as my heavenly parents, and they have never let me down, especially in my darkest hours. They have always been there for me, and I would find deep consolation in them. I would tell them all my childhood

19

problems and worries. To me, my statues were real; I loved them because they were symbolic of Heaven, another world where a beautiful life force existed. This world was full of angels that represented a beautiful, mysterious, mystical, and spiritual love that penetrates the earth. I could never imagine my life without my beautiful heavenly friends.

I loved my own mother beyond words. She was a gentle soul and a wonderful person. I am very grateful to her for telling me all the wonderful stories about Our Lady and the saints. Heaven was my escape from earthly strife. I liked the fact that my heavenly friends were unreachable and lived in another world called Heaven. I would kneel on the floor in my bedroom and pray the rosary, and I made sure I never left anyone out, especially the poor souls in Purgatory. That was a big one; I would make some sacrifices whenever I could at that young age. Sometimes, I would try to refuse my food as a small sacrifice for sinners to enable souls to get into Heaven, but that would upset my father. Needless to say, the plan didn't last too long.

"Every block of stone has a statue inside of it and it is the task of the sculptor to discover it."- Michelangelo

# Chapter 6

## My Friend Rene

*Rene was my childhood friend, and we are still friends to this day.* We were in the same classes all through school and remained friends afterward. We will always be friends, and she knows all about my heavenly experiences.

Sometimes, she will ask me, "Have you ever see your vision again? Did he ever come back to see you?"

I always reply, "No, not yet."

However, she also knows about my heavenly experiences over here in America, too, and without question, my friend Rene believes me because she knows me. She always asks me to pray for her, and I assure her that she is on my prayer list.

PRAYER

A Friend Is a Gift of God

"Among the great and glorious gifts our heavenly Father sends

Is the gift of Understanding that we find in loving friends

For in this world of trouble that is filled with anxious care

Everybody needs a friend…"

—St. Margaret Mary's

Canon B Devine

# Chapter 7

## My Cousin Peggy

*Sometimes after Mass, I would go up to visit my cousin Peggy.*
She would tease me and ask, "Nancy, have you been to chapel, booking your wings for Heaven?"

We would laugh at that. I loved her; she was so full of life, and she had a great sense of humor. She was an amazing person and had a wonderful, large family. I'm sure it was rough on her, but she never complained because she made the best of life.

There was never a dull moment at Peggy's house. Neighbors and friends were always popping in for a cup of tea and a chat especially after Sunday Mass.

Peggy has since passed on, and she is sorely missed by her beloved family. But, I am sure that God was waiting for her with a special set of wings.

# PRAYER

## *Memorare*

"Remember, O most gracious Virgin Mary, that never was it known that anyone who fled to your protection, implored your help, or sought your intercession was left unaided. Inspired by your confidence, I fly unto you, O Virgin of virgins, my Mother. To you I come; before you I stand sinful and sorrowful. O Mother of the Word Incarnate! Despise not my petitions, but in your mercy hear and answer me. Amen.

# Chapter 8

## Saint Theresa and Saint Anthony

*I considered Saint Theresa the little flower, my friend, and she* was a good influence in my life. I tried to live like the saints and was deeply inspired by them. I loved to get lost in their lives, especially the little flower, who was my spiritual childhood friend and who still is my spiritual friend. I have a small picture of her from my childhood, and in spite of moving around the world over the years, I haven't lost it. I will always treasure it because it's a part of my past.

Let us go forward in peace,
our eyes upon Heaven,
the only one goal
of our labors
   St.Therese of the Child Jesus.

I could never have made it in life without dear Saint Anthony. He has helped me out of many a situation and has come to my aid many times. Saint Anthony is known as the wonder worker. If somebody has lost something important, the faithful recite this very short Irish prayer, which is still widely used to this day because it works: "Saint Anthony, please come around; something is lost, and must be found."

PRAYER

"O Holy Saint Anthony, gentlest of saints, your love for God and charity for His creatures made you worthy when on earth to possess miraculous powers. Encouraged by this thought, I implore you to obtain for me my request for healing. O gentle and loving St. Anthony, whose heart was ever full of human sympathy, whisper my petition into the ears of the sweet Infant Jesus, who loved to be folded in your arms; will ever be yours. Amen."

# Chapter 9

## The Brilliant Light
## on the Battlefield

My father was a soldier in the Royal Artillery Army. I know he saw many horrific things over there in France. He seldom talked about it, but it was obvious that it bothered him, because some of his friends died on the battlefields in Normandy. However, I remember my father did tell me about one time when he and his buddies from the regiment were at the front lines, when suddenly a large, brilliant, mysterious light from the sky enveloped them and blinded them, making it impossible for them to see anything or to move forward. This brilliant, mysterious light stopped them from crossing over to the other side where the enemy was lying in wait for them. My father only talked about this experience if I pressured him; otherwise, he would never discuss the war or his experiences, but I do know that he suffered terribly from the war.

This brilliant light was seen all over Europe on January 25–26, 1938, and I'm sure it was the great sign promised by Our Lady to Sister Lucia of Fatima.

PRAYER

"The Lord is my light and my salvation; whom shall I fear? The Lord is the stronghold of my life; of whom shall I be afraid…Though an army encamps against me, my heart shall not fear. The light of God surrounds me; the love of God enfolds me; the power of God protects me; the presence of God watches over me; wherever I am, God is."

—James Dillet Freeman

# Part 2

## The Time Has Come

*My deep love for Our Lady goes way back to my early* childhood and probably stems from another love—my love of books. I spent endless hours reading anything I could find—especially in the Bible—anything that contained the amazing life story of Jesus and also the stories of Jesus and the apostles. They brought the Holy Bible to life, along with all the characters and those true heroes who endured all sorts of setbacks and even death because of their faith in God.

Even early in my life, I had a deep respect for books, but it was never my intention to write one. I was just happy reading them. Of course, that all changed after one fantastic, incredible winter's night when I had a most beautiful and mystical supernatural experience. I consider such an experience a very rare privilege that few people, if any at all, ever have. The encounter that I and my two nurse friends experienced was definitely from the other side, from Heaven. It will remain imprinted in my brain forever, and I will carry it with me to the other world.

I have thought very hard and have prayed very deeply to God to guide me in writing this book, releasing something to the public that I have kept under wraps for years.

# Chapter 10

## The Time Has Come

*It has been said that once Our Lady gets hold of you, she never* lets you go. So now I will go ahead and share my experiences with the divine supernatural in a book that I never thought of writing but have decided to write after much thought and many prayers. I want to share my supernatural experiences to help people realize that they are in very serious danger of losing their souls. As a Catholic, I feel that it is one's duty to care for the soul, to nourish and protect it, and to guide it on the path toward its final destination. In this world, it's all about the soul and how one lives one's life according to God's plan.

Looking back to that very special night of my divine encounter with the most Holy Blessed Mother and the holy angel Numinous, I learned that humans are not in control of this world at all. Man is not in control of anything down here on this earth, even though at the moment it might certainly seem that way. Most of our leaders are sadly lacking in faith and lacking in belief. They have been weakened by the materialistic way of life and no longer have the strength to resist all the temptations of this world. God is in control.

In the introduction, I said I had never thought of writing a book—that is, until after one winter's night in late 1993, just before Christmas, when something very wonderful and most unexpected and supernatural happened that pierced the very foundation of my soul and changed my life in an instant. It led me to reach out to the Catholic Church for help because I desperately needed answers and explanations, and most importantly, I needed to give the Church this message from God.

This is very hard; I've had lots of setbacks. But I have to persist past the retreat of my friends and the refusal of various priests I've talked to. At the same time, I fully understand that the hierarchy has to be extremely cautious in these delicate matters regarding the supernatural, and I stand by them in their decision to protect the reputation of the Church.

I was born into the Catholic faith and raised by my family in the teachings of the Catholic Church; these teachings are a part of me and always will be. I have waited patiently and trod very carefully, not wanting to go against the Church. One very special priest told me I have a mission, and I believe that is to tell my story. And the best way for me to do this is to put my divine experience in a book so that I can bring it to people's attention. This might help and inspire them, and most importantly, give people hope and let them know that we are definitely not alone in the universe.

I feel the time has come for me to let the good people of this city and the world know what happened here that night on a quiet side street off the beaten path of a very busy and bustling city, where life whizzes by at one hundred miles a minute. Trusting in the protection of God, I will begin my story. Through the power of God, I will tell how this unknown and insignificant little street was magnificently transformed into a glorious piece of Heaven right here in the heart of Hell's Kitchen, New York City, which has become my piece of sacred ground. As for the other two women who were with me that special night, they wish to remain in hiding, keeping their heads in the sand, hoping it will all go away.

It won't.

Watch and pray, lest you enter into temptation. The spirit indeed is willing, but the flesh is weak.

Mark 14:38

# Chapter 11

## My Story

*As I mentioned in the previous chapter, it was an encounter so* profound that it shook the very foundation of my soul and led me to reach out to the Catholic Church for help. Because of the importance of what had taken place, I really needed feedback and explanations, but the clergy were not sure what to do. But there were a couple of good priests who were willing to listen and try to help me.

However, years are going by, and nothing is getting done, and people are falling deeper into sin and darkness. Many people, especially young people, are dying needlessly way before their time. This is why I have decided to continue on and write this book and tell what happened that night that concerns everyone in this world.

It was on a bitter cold winter's night late in December 1993, a Friday; the time was around 8:45 p.m. I was taking courses at Seton College, which was used as an extension of Iona College. The semester was almost finished, and we were busy with exams. Christmas was fast approaching. At that time, I was staying at a hotel on the West side of Manhattan, not far from the college, while waiting to move into a new apartment on the Upper East Side of Manhattan. I was happy and excited, because at the end of this semester, I was going to visit my sister May and my two nephews who lived in Canada. My sister was suffering from breast cancer, but she was strong and had the best doctors, and she seemed to be doing fine. However, sadly, this would be our last Christmas together. I really missed her and could not wait to see her. I had my plane ticket, and I was all packed and ready to go. It was all good.

I had just finished a class on death and dying. Little did I know that I was about to get a real lesson on life and death within the next thirty minutes because something so dramatic and wonderful, yet scary, was about to happen that would change my life forever. I would never be the same or think about life the same way as before or take life for granted ever again.

# Chapter 12

# The Heavenly Blue Globe

*I was waiting for my classmates Sheila and Roslyn.* Once they arrived, we began walking along West Thirty-Third Street toward Ninth Avenue. As we passed the large statue of the Sacred Heart of Jesus, I stopped as I always did and said a prayer. The statue is part of Saint Michael's Roman Catholic Church, which is adjacent to a parking lot. Something drew my attention toward the left side of the sky. As I looked up, I noticed a very large object. It was a very unusual, beautiful color of blue; at first, I thought it was a cloud, but quickly realized it was a globe or possibly a planet standing majestically against the backdrop of a black sky, diagonally above Saint Michael's Church. The time was roughly 8:45 p.m.

I called out, "Oh! Look at that!"

Sheila and I walked quickly down the little driveway leading into the parking lot to have a closer look at this awe-inspiring vision.

Sheila said, "What is that?" As we got closer, she cried out, "Oh, my God!"

We both stood there in amazement as the planet-like globe began to loosen from the sky and descend toward the earth, coming down to meet us. The next minute, it was suspended in midair about ten or fifteen feet above us at a comfortable level. It was massive, roughly 800 hundred feet, or more, in diameter, and it covered the entire apartment building.

Instantly, we were drawn into a time warp and into another dimension. It commanded our attention and was of extreme importance and not of this world. It was majestic, magnificent, graceful, and mysterious, and had a very powerful presence that spoke volumes. We were standing quite close to it for a few minutes, and then it quickly changed formation from a perfectly round globe into an oblong shape.

I was taking mental notes because all my writing materials—pen, paper, and notebook and my rosary beads —were in my backpack; besides, there was no time now because it was all happening so fast. If this planet-like globe were symbolic of our world, the message I seemed to be getting was that more than half of our world would soon be gone. This was the message I was picking up from my instincts and observations along with telepathic thoughts that seemed to point to the epicenter of our world. I could see in this globe that there was no sky or clouds or vegetation or any form of life. It was just a beautiful, rare color of blue—the wholly other, highly charged wonderfulness of Grace.

Suddenly, the dimensions changed; our surroundings moved back and expanded, like a new filming technique, in preparation for what was to come next. I could no longer see the apartment buildings or Saint Michael's Church. Now we were definitely in another dimension, and earthly time stood still; we were outside of our time. I was so engrossed in this strange and beautiful yet scary encounter, and from that moment onward, I was oblivious to everything in our world and was even unaware of Sheila standing next to me for a short period of time.

It seemed to me that this heavenly globe was symbolic of our world, and it was going to change dramatically and very rapidly. It was going to take a turn for the worse.

The world would soon become unrecognizable. We are in trouble.

This was the first vision.  We saw a blue globe
illuminated by the light from the tree.

The blue globe flipped and morphed into a long oblong
shape.

# Chapter 13

## A Second Vision of an Apocalyptic Nature

### Preparatory Vision

*Suddenly, an invisible and unknown force gently and very slowly*
turned me around toward a large tree on which there was an
outline of a being. This being was between six and ten feet
in height, possibly taller; transparent; and shining with
pure, brilliant, supernatural, and unapproachable light. The
figure was dazzling as though large, shimmering diamonds
or sparkling stars were coming from within, without, and
all around her. At first glance, she seemed to be hovering,
as if to gain balance, and she blended through the tree and
yet was supported by standing on a heavenly cloud that was
pure and thick.

I cried out, "Oh, look!" I moved closer toward the
tree, with Sheila a couple of steps behind me. At first, I was

a bit frustrated and wondered why I couldn't see her face, even though it was a cold winter's night and the branches were barren of leaves. Just as I was thinking this, her face materialized from pixilated to clear; her eyes were black- it was as if she had read my thoughts. However, once the vision fully manifested, it then rapidly changed to another vision of a divine angel from Heaven. This angel was full of purely supernatural power—strong, vibrant, and overwhelming—and was of an apocalyptic nature and definitely from another world.

The divine angel in the vision was a warrior of great celestial power and beauty beyond description. She was all business, as if ready for battle. At first, she was standing throughout the tree, at a higher level. Instantly, she became larger and in full focus, yet still stayed in the same spot on the tree. It was as if the vision projected itself directly in front of me, face-to-face, to make sure that I received the message. And the message was not good.

That was when I realized that we were in serious trouble down here on earth. The expression on the angel's face was deadly serious and very somber. I was very afraid. The angel let me know that she was sent by God for one purpose only, and that was to give humankind a warning of what was coming to the world. I was able to pick up the angel's message in three ways: telepathically, from her facial expression, and from a feeling that was very definite and final. This beautiful angel let me know that God was not happy with the people down here on earth and that the world was about to change forever. Although there was no eye contact between us, instinctively I knew this was not good and that we were in serious trouble and imminent danger.

She looked like a statue, eyes, had changed to clear white- with her hands folded in a prayerful posture. Her head was slightly tilted upward, and she raised her eyes, upward to Heaven and at the same time was peering far into the distance, as if looking years into the future or into another dimension. I tried to follow the divine angel's gaze, but it was impossible because she was at a higher level than we were, and she was looking past Saint Michael's Church in the direction of Eleventh Avenue and the Hudson River. The angel did not associate herself with us, except to let us know that the angel's duty as the messenger of God was to give this message along with the warning that God was not happy with the people down here and that He was very much offended by the way we are living our lives. We must repent and do penance. And pray.

I was able to pick up the message and interpret it, and most importantly, I was able to understand the message, which was that death and destruction were coming to this city and would quickly spread all over the world—the contents of the message were not good. There would be a great loss of faith and a great loss of life. I knew from the divine angel that night that the world was about to change forever; it would *never* be the same again. We are in terrible trouble and existential danger!

I realized the divine angel's mission was strictly to give me this message of warning. Her mission was accomplished.


"A bleak prophesy of death and destruction."

Prophesy shows the reliability of the Scriptures, which do not come from men but are sent by God.

2 Peter 1:19-21, ESV.


"Angels are spirits, but it is not because they are spirits that they are angels. They become angels when they are sent, for the name angel refers to their office, not their nature.

You ask the name of this nature, it is spirit; you ask its office. It is that of an angel, which a messenger is."

—Saint Augustine

# Chapter 14

# A Third Vision: A True Queen from Heaven

*Once the angel's mission was accomplished, in a split-second, the scene* changed dramatically. There was a flurry of invisible activity at the tree. At this point, I could actually feel the irises of my eyes, especially my left eye. My pupils had contracted and altered in size, as if the retinas had changed without my control to adjust to what was taking place in front of me.

To the best of my knowledge, I will try to explain what followed next. Suddenly and swiftly, another vision came into focus where the first vision of the angel previously stood. I could now see another vision inside, a side profile of a tall and slender lady who was wearing a long, pure-white dress, with her head and upper part of her body slightly leaning forward in a maternal and prayerful posture, similar to the image of Our Lady of Fatima. This vision seemed to glide or fly rapidly along the side of Saint

Michael's Church, coming straight toward me. I could feel my eyes open wide, especially my left eye. Now the vision was in close proximity, but not within my personal space, nor within touching distance. I was taking the full brunt of this vision because she definitely knew me and wanted to communicate with me. The supreme, spiritual being had moved away from the tree and was now facing Saint Michael's Church, still midway in the sky. It is hard to gauge distance when you are faced with a divine vision from God, because you are completely taken over by the magnitude and the amplification of the real presence of a true Divine Queen from another dimension.

Now the vision was standing upon a massive, pure-white, thick heavenly cloud that was vibrant, very much alive, and full of purely spiritual power with machinelike propulsion that seemed to defy gravity—or should I say was in command of gravity. This heavenly cloud was very powerful and not from our world, but from another world altogether.

Standing upon this heavenly cloud was the most beautiful lady I have ever seen in my life. This lady was a true Queen from another world. She was named Numinous, which means the "wholly other." She was tall and slender and leaned slightly forward with an expression of such exceptional tenderness. I cannot explain her beauty, as I have nothing on earth to compare her with; she was incomparable to anyone or anything in this world. She was indeed a real, True Celestial Queen from another kingdom that I can only assume must be Heaven.

The Lady wore a long, plain eggshell-white dress of the finest of very delicate silk. It was very simple but elegant and regal with a high, round neck with long sleeves that were tapered at the wrists. The Lady also wore a long eggshell-white veil over her head, reaching all the way down to her feet, with brilliant lights emanating from within and without and all around her. She was all of pure, vibrant light and was surrounded by a light-gray grotto that had manifested around her and seemed to me to reflect Our Lady of Fatima and Our Lady of Lourdes.

The Lady was most gracious, divinely humble, and dignified. She then joined her hands together in prayer; her hands seemed to sink deep into the center of the diaphragm toward the sternum. I had the distinct feeling that she, the Lady, was going to open up the now-expanded ground and show me something. At the same time, she was smiling at me ever so maternally and so very sincerely, with such an outpouring of love. Such purity; she was so pure, I was not afraid. On the contrary, I felt joyful, and it all seemed so perfectly natural to me. My mind was working overtime as I tried to take in every detail that my mind could consume of this most beautiful vision that could only have come from Heaven. She was so clean and pure and definitely not from our world—the *Numinous*, the *Mysterium Tremendum*.

She had the most beautiful blue eyes, bluer than the sky. We had direct eye-to-eye contact, unlike the first vision of the angel where there had been no eye contact between us; the angel had seemed to be looking at me yet through me to make sure I received the message. But, with the beautiful Lady it was different. At that precise moment, I could feel with every fiber in my body that the Lady and I were preparing to communicate with each other, and I was preparing to ask her questions, when suddenly a voice pierced the cold, dark night. It was Roslyn.

"Come on, I have to catch my train, and I'm cold. It's freezing standing here."

Keeping my eyes transfixed on the vision of the Lady, I walked over to Roslyn, remembering from my childhood the stories about Fatima and Lourdes and how Our Lady the Blessed Mother had always identified herself. Walking slowly toward Roslyn, and still full of this magical, mystical, and joyful feeling, I said, "Roslyn, this is very important." With my eyes still fully focused on the vision of the beautiful Lady, I said, "This could be the Blessed Mother."

Roslyn replied, with a smile, "I know."

After Roslyn said that, the Lady did not acknowledge or disavow any hint of her identity. However, by this time, I was convinced that this was indeed the Blessed Mother who definitely looked like a taller version of Our Lady of Fatima! This was the same Lady whom I had learned about throughout my childhood through the love of my parents. She was a part of our family, a very special part of the family; of course, I loved her and had always prayed to her and depended on her throughout my life. I considered her to be my Heavenly Mother who lived far, far away, in another world called Heaven, and I could call upon her anytime for help. I knew her before I knew the world. And now here she was, standing right in front of me on a massive, pure-white heavenly cloud, suspended in the air against the force of gravity.

This beautiful vision of Our Lady—words cannot describe her beauty, and words cannot describe how I felt at those timeless moments. Never in my wildest dreams did I ever expect to see Our Lady in my lifetime. We were in the heavenly presence of a real, Celestial Queen.

I said to Roslyn again that this was very important; this could be the Blessed Mother.

Roslyn replied, "Yes I know, but I have to get my train. I have to get home to the kids."

While we were having this discussion about Roslyn's eagerness to get home to her family, I was very conscious of Our Lady waiting patiently and listening. The atmosphere around us was electrifying and very dramatic. All of my senses were on super-high-alert. My eyes were frantically darting from Roslyn then back to Our Lady because I did not want to lose focus of the vision that by now seemed to be on the left side of my peripheral view. The vision seemed to move along beside me—along with Sheila still tagging along behind me—and did not murmur one word.

Roslyn was facing me, and I now realized that she was not seeing the vision of Our Lady or sharing in the same experiences that Sheila and I were. For some reason, Roslyn was not allowed to see the visions of Our Lady and the angelic angel, but I do know that she did see the first vision of the blue planet- like globe that to me seemed to be symbolic of the earth. Roslyn had not come into the driveway next to Saint Michael's Church because she was afraid. So there I was, caught between the physical and the spiritual in a tug-of-war between the spiritual and the physical worlds.

I am not sure what happened next. I was trying to be considerate to Roslyn and at the same time not lose focus of the vision of Our Lady. But why we allowed Roslyn to steer us away from this heavenly encounter that divine night, unless the presence of God was so powerful, I'll never know and have always regretted.

And perhaps the visions of Our Lady and the angel were so strong that they took away our bodily senses, and therefore I could not think logically. This was all beyond my understanding; it did not make any sense. One minute we were walking and chatting, and the next minute— completely out of nowhere with no warning—here we were the three of us, suddenly caught up in a time warp! And thrust into another dimension that was not of this world, but in a completely different world! It was magical, mystical, mysterious, unreal, and yet so very real. None of it made sense at the time. So we just turned and left.

This was not like me; nothing would have dragged me away from that spot. I was trying to be considerate to Roslyn and also to this beautiful vision of Our Lady. As I have said before, I was torn between the spiritual and the physical. I cannot seem to forgive myself for leaving the way we did. Perhaps that's the way it was meant to be, and we had no control over the situation. All I know is this beautiful Lady, all of pure, brilliant light and pure love, took a part of me with her, and my life will never be the same.

On that same night we made our way to the train station in deep silence. I was so overcome by the magnitude of what had just happened because it was so strong and overwhelming. Roslyn walked to another station to catch her train to Brooklyn. I accompanied Sheila toward the Thirty-Fourth Street Station to catch her train to Queens.

As we stood on the platform waiting for her train to come into the station, she looked at me and remarked, "It's just you and me against the world; no one will believe us."

And with a sigh, I replied, "Yes, I know."

However, later on the following week after giving some thought to Sheila's apprehension in coming forward as witness to this divine event. It now looks like; it's only me against the world, I hope with a team of heavenly angels around me, because I am going to need all of the heavenly help I can get. I remember thinking that it was a very cold night and she—Our Lady—must have been cold because she was only wearing a dress, and why did she appear outside Saint Michael's Church? And was the angel there in the tree to begin with, or is it possible that when the planet-like globe changed formation that's when the angel chose that tree to hold the vision of Our Lady? I know this visitation was planned by God, and it did not just happen by chance. As, Bishop Fulton Sheen said "Nothing ever happens out of heaven except with a finesse of all details; The vision of Our Lady was also a message of hope, and whatever is coming to the world through death and destruction, she would take care of all her children. I trust her with my life in this world and the next one.

## THE WOMAN CLOTHED WITH THE SUN

"And a great sign appeared in heaven: A woman clothed with the sun and the moon under her feet and on her head a crown of twelve stars."__ Apocalypse 12: 1

And there appeared another wonder in heaven; and behold a Great Red Dragon..._ Apocalypse 12: 3

# Chapter 15

## Angel of the Apocalypse

*The Catholic tradition regards Saint Michael the Archangel as* the defender and protector of the Church and of individual Christians. As a champion of God's people and a patron of various medieval orders of knights, he is often depicted as having a sword in his hand. His other insignia is the scales of justice, because he is the one who executes the decision on each person's eternal destiny on Judgment Day.

Saint Michael, who ranks among the seven archangels, is also one of the three angels mentioned by name in the scriptures. Saint Michael is spoken of four times in scriptures. In chapter 12 of the book of Revelation, Saint John recounts his vision of the great battle in Heaven, when the wicked angels under Lucifer revolted against God, and how Michael, leading the faithful angels as prince of the seraphim, overcomes the dragon. The Apocalypse is a revelation of things that were, are, and will be. We are actually witnessing some of the events foretold in this book, but many still lie in the future. It was Christ who commanded John to write to the seven churches, opened the seven seals, revealed the sufferings of the saints, and opened the little book. It is Christ who will overcome the beast, reign during the period of the first resurrection, and judge the dead at His second coming. It is Christ who rules over all things from the beginning, presides over all the changing scenes of earth's history, and is the King of kings and Lord of lords.

The book of Saint John the Apostle presents Christ as the coming one; it reveals the dealings of Him who came, and who is to come. It opens with the solemn hope that the coming one will come soon and closes with the impressive prediction that the coming one will come quickly. The book is one of hope, but also one of warning.

"Fear not: for, behold, I bring you good tidings of great joy."

—Luke 2: 10

\*\*\*

The fact that God chose to include Saint Michael's Church in Our Lady's visitation here on earth proves that Saint Michael's Church was chosen by God himself. And Saint

Michael is mentioned in the book of Revelation as the warrior prince and defender of the Church. The great clash that John speaks of that will occur at the end of time also reflects the battle in Heaven at the beginning of time, when Satan and his devotees were defeated and banished from Heaven.

God has mercifully concealed from us the day and the hour when this dreaded event shall occur. Our Lord himself said to his disciples, "But that day and hour no one knows, not even the Angels of Heaven, but the Father only. And as it was in the days of Noe, even so will be the coming of the Son of Man. For as in the days before the flood, they were eating and drinking, marrying and giving in marriage until the day when Noe entered the ark, and they did not understand until the flood came and swept them all away; even so will be the coming of the Son of Man" (Mt 24:36–38). Nevertheless, our Lord foretold certain signs that would precede the end of the world and be a warning of its approach. These signs are described in chapter 24 of the Gospel of Saint Matthew. After describing the terrors of the end of the world of this final battle when the end of the world draws near, Saint Michael will wage a final battle against the antichrist, which will perform false miracles and engage in frightful persecutions.

This is foretold in Daniel 12:1, where the prophet, speaking of the end of the world and the antichrist, says, "At that time Michael shall rise up, the great prince, who standeth for the children of thy people! And a time shall come such as never was from the time that nations began even until that time. And at that time shall thy people be saved, everyone that shall be found written in the book."

"And there was a great battle in heaven; Michael and his angels fought with the dragon, and the dragon fought and his angels. And they did not prevail, neither was their place found anymore in heaven. And that great dragon was cast down, the ancient serpent, who is called the devil and Satan, who leads astray the whole world; and he was cast down to the earth and with him his angels were cast down." (Apoc. 12:7–9)

After this most valiant archangel has once conquered the prince of darkness and has cast him into the abyss of Hell, he will sound the trumpet whose resonance will call the dead to life and summon all men before the eternal judge to receive their final sentence of reward or punishment. Happy shall we be if in that awful hour we find an advocate in the glorious Archangel Michael! Let us always be faithful in invoking him.

Irish people have always held Michael, the captain of the heavenly host, in great veneration, as is evident from the number of ancient churches dedicated to him and with the frequency that his name is given to their children. They termed him *Adrigh na Aaingeal*, or "the High King of the Angels."

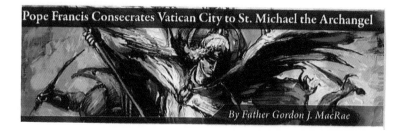

Pope Francis Consecrates Vatican City to St. Michael the Archangel

*By Father Gordon J. MacRae*

These Stone Walls:
"For, he will give his angels charge of you to guard you in all your ways. On their hands they will bear you up, lest you dash your foot against a stone."

(Psalm 91:11-12)

# Chapter 16

## Lunch at the Cheyenne Diner

*A few weeks later, I met Sheila for lunch at the Cheyenne Diner,* a place which plays a large part in the story. We discussed what had happened on that special night and what we had both experienced. I proceeded to bring out my notes and sketches that detailed what we had experienced a few weeks ago.

Sheila seemed surprised and exclaimed, "You have done all this?"

"Well, yes," I replied, spreading on the table my notes of what I had seen and experienced on that night of this very important and heavenly encounter with the divine supernatural. Holding up the sketch of the vision of Our Lady, I asked her, "Is this what you saw? See (Appendix A.)

Looking at the drawing, she lowered her head and quietly whispered, "Yes." She also told me that she had the date of that night in her diary. I only wished that I had asked for it. I gave her a set of rosary beads and a little prayer book

Fingering the rosary beads, she asked me, "Are there support groups for people who have seen apparitions?"

"No, Sheila," I replied, "this was more than an apparition; this was the real thing. This was a visitation from the Blessed Mother herself, a True Celestial Queen of the angels from Heaven, and I think it is better if you don't talk about this to anyone except the church authorities. Just pray and say the rosary every day, sincerely, like Our Lady always requests."

I suggested that we should really report it to the church authorities as soon as possible, because it was far too important and far above us to ignore it. We both agreed to go to the archdiocese. However, the following week on the morning when we were to go and talk to the priest, Sheila backed out at the last minute. I am guessing that she was afraid of coming forward and actually talking to the hierarchy of the archdiocese, so I would have to continue and follow through with this mission on my own, relying on much help from God!

Sheila had also thought that other people must have seen the same thing, meaning the blue globe/planet on that night. But if no one could see it except me and the other two nurses who were with me, that meant it was invisible to the world, and therefore Sheila and I had been the only ones allowed to see it in person and approach it. I do know one thing: these two girls were with me for the simple reason to bear witness and to attest to what happened that night, but it was really meant for me to tell the world. It's taken so long because I was waiting for the Catholic Church to do something positive, and I have finally realized that they are not going to do anything. And I also realize this message is not only for Catholics; it is for everyone in the world.

The angel had let me know that the world was in deep trouble, and God was not happy at all with humankind. Man was deteriorating rapidly; a great loss of faith and life would come, and the world would fall and change dramatically. Since that night, the world has fallen mightily, and sadly, it continues to fall at frightening speed. But after what I saw and experienced that night, I cannot just forget and continue on with my life as if nothing ever happened. On the contrary, something of major importance did happen, and it concerns the future of humankind. I have a responsibility to let people know. Now I stood alone, without Sheila and Roslyn; it's not easy, but it has to be done.

One's life is never quite the same after an encounter with the divine from Heaven.

"Every visible thing in this world is put in the charge of an Angel."

Saint Augustine

"Make yourself familiar with the angels, and behold them frequently in spirit; for without being seen, they are present with you."

St. Francis De Sales.

# Chapter 17

## A Visit to the Archdiocese

*It was about one week later in December when I called Monsignor* Falishione of Saint Michael's Roman Catholic Church to tell him what had happened because it concerned his church. He advised me to keep going back to the tree and said that I should also go to the Chancery. At that time, I was not sure what and where the Chancery was, but I thanked him anyway, not taking into consideration that he would not believe me; after all, he was a priest. Later on, I learned from someone that he actually did not believe me and stated that he heard those stories every day. That saddened me because it just did not occur to me that people would not believe me.

So I made an appointment to go to the archdiocese because I was scared, not only for myself but also for the future of the world. Besides, I needed answers and help from the Catholic Church. Were they not the experts? Surely they would help me. I made a phone call to the Archdiocese of Manhattan and gave Monsignor O'Donnell a brief synopsis of what had happened that night, telling him that we had had a very unique experience. I sensed that he did not really grasp what I was saying to him on the phone because I was being very discreet and careful with my words. The monsignor asked me to bring in the girls. Then Sheila backed out at the last minute, so I went alone.

As I was going up in the elevator to meet the monsignor, a sudden thought came to me: "The higher up you go, the dirtier it will become." Where did that thought come from? It could only have come from God via an angel messenger gently warning me to be careful.

The monsignor was waiting for me and led me into a conference room that held a large, deep mahogany, highly polished table surrounded by matching chairs. He pulled out a chair for me. I thanked him, suddenly feeling a bit unsure of myself now that I was facing this priest at the other end of this huge conference table. But I was here now, and there was no turning back. Besides, it was not about me; it was about Our Lady and her message from God for the world.

We exchanged brief, cordial introductions. He asked about the other two girls and whether they were coming. I explained that they were not coming. Then I handed him the document containing my notes pertaining to that divine night. I watched him carefully as he read it intensely. His face formed a look of shock and disbelief. He folded his hands across his arms as if he had goose bumps, then he slid down halfway off his chair. He was clearly affected by what he was reading.

I almost asked him, "Are you all right, Father?" I wish now that I had. Obviously, this was not the kind of story he was expecting to hear; he was completely unprepared for this. This was too close to home for comfort—it was in his backyard. It would have been better if it had been thousands of miles away in another country.

The monsignor looked directly at me, and trying to recover from this unusual meeting, he asked me, "Has this ever happened to you before?"

I replied, "Yes, once when I was a child, I had a vision of Jesus."

After the meeting and while waiting for the elevator to come, I glanced over toward the monsignor; it was clear to me that he was in a quandary and was trying to grasp what he had just read. A few weeks went by, and there was no word from Monsignor O'Donnell, so I sent him a letter and thanked him for at least seeing me. There was still no feedback—nothing. Little did I know that this was to be the beginning of paper trails and visits to different priests and churches as I tried to get the message out? Not giving up and with a driving force pushing me on, I was relentless in my mission.

Father McCartney was a dear priest from Saint Francis Roman Catholic Church on West Thirty-First Street in Manhattan who also hailed from Scotland. In the past we met for lunch a couple of times because we had a lot in common, Scotland being our homeland. Father McCartney had at one time mentioned that I should see Monsignor Clark and have a word with him because he was very conservative, and he also loved Our Lady, and he might be able to help me in some way. He also advised me not to say anything to people in general and that Our Lady wanted me to be close to her son, Jesus.

Even though I loved Father McCartney's answer, and it made me happy that Our Lady wanted me to be near Jesus, in my heart I knew that this encounter with Our Lady and the angel meant much more. It could not possibly be about the three of us. No, it was much more serious than that, a far bigger picture with devastating consequences that were about to follow. Our Lady was not going to let me off the hook this easily. If there is anything in this life I have learned about Our Lady, it is that she does not give up easily, and she is gently persistent until the mission is accomplished. Since I was the only messenger at this time and was still available and willing, I would do my very best, and more, if required. I was a lot spiritually stronger, and I realized that I could not let this fade into the background of time. It's simply too important and relevant to our time.

But I was completely on my own in this mission.

# Chapter 18

## Monsignor Clark

*Finally, I made an appointment with Monsignor Clark at Saint* Agnes Roman Catholic Church, which is one of my favorite churches. Monsignor Clark was a very eloquent and highly intelligent priest and was a tremendous fund-raiser for the diocese. He always had a ready smile to greet you. He was an extraordinary priest. Out of the few priests I went to for help and guidance, he was the only priest who took me in and was the most helpful. He listened most graciously to what I had to say.

"Ah! I see you have taken some notes. Good."

While giving the good priest my notes, I related my story to him. "Father, they do exist. She is alive and is unearthly beautiful. I cannot find anything on this earth to compare her to; I have seen her up close. This was an invisible and unreachable supernatural vision of the Blessed Virgin Mary, whom I have been praying to all my life. I have been giving her all my problems and sufferings of life, especially for other poor souls in this world and the souls in Purgatory. She was standing directly in front of me, Face-to-face. After all these years of searching and reading every book I could find about her, especially the little Fatima books, I had always considered her my heavenly mother. She finally revealed herself and made herself visible to me, as if to say, 'I am aware of you, and I love you, and you are not alone!'"

Monsignor Clark was calm, collected, and very interested as he scanned over my notes and sketches.

I said, "Father Clark, this is such a difficult task, and I cannot understand why Our Lady would choose such an awkward place to come to. It doesn't make any sense to me. There is a driveway and a space that is used for parked cars, and close by is an apartment building and two restaurants, and a few steps away stands the church of Saint Michael's.

The monsignor smiled and replied, "Oh, Our Lady does not worry about things like that. An apartment building is not going to stop her." Then Monsignor Clark asked, "Where, exactly, is this place?"

I answered, "It's on West Thirty-Third Street between Ninth and Eleventh Avenues, near Saint Michael's Roman Catholic Church."

Monsignor Clark continued. "What are the other two girls' names?"

I replied, "Their names are Sheila and Roslyn."

Monsignor Clark followed with, "If you did see Our Lady as you say—"

"When I think of that night and the intimacy of the encounter, because it was so sacred, so divine, so real, and so very important, and when I think of the reality of that night, I am elated and honored, but I am also very afraid, not so much for myself but for the future of the world. The vision seemed to project, to emphasize the angel's expression on her face, which was very grave. She looked like a warrior, all of supernatural power. I knew immediately that the vision of the angel was letting me know that God is not happy with us down here on earth and that we are still in very serious trouble and in imminent danger. The vision of the angel warrior was of an apocalyptic nature. The world was going to go through dramatic changes through the destruction and deterioration of man and a great loss of faith. The world would become much smaller than it is now." Monsignor Clark listened carefully and advised me to be patient, and again he repeated, "If you did see Our Lady as you say, I believe you; I believe that she came to give you the message."

"Monsignor Clark, I don't want to be a visionary. I am a very private person, and I couldn't bear people watching me, praying, and following me like a curiosity."

The Monsignor shot back, "You have no choice!"

"What I really meant to say was if I am to be a visionary, then I would want to be a good visionary and an honest one, and not to be put into a category of false visionaries who make up stories for many reasons. I find this diabolical and would never associate myself with anything deceitful concerning the true faith! Especially the Blessed Mother; that would surely offend God!"

But the truth is I am a true visionary; I was born with the gift from God. It's important for people to know and understand that the Blessed Mother of Jesus did indeed come to this country and straight into the heart of New York City, simply because she knew that we would need her. She also warned us of the dangers that lay ahead for America and the world.

Monsignor Clark thanked me and mentioned that I should try and bring the girls in to see him. I thanked him for his time and promised that I would indeed try and that I would keep in touch with him.

A few days later, I called Monsignor Clark and explained that I could not bring in the girls to talk with him.

Sheila said she was not coming forward because she was afraid, and she felt that other people had also seen something. I know that what happened that night had scared them. Looking back on, that very special divine night when I was alone and all was quiet, and I thought of the reality of what had happened earlier that night, I was very much afraid myself, knowing that there really is another life force, the wholly other that does exist and is very much alive and far more superior than we could ever hope to be. And now that these girls were afraid to come forward, I would have to continue alone, and this could only make my task more difficult. So I knew where I stood and that I was on my own in this mission. It was the way it had to be.

Monsignor Clark was very careful, and I am not sure if he believed me immediately, which I can now understand. At first, it never occurred to me that there would be a problem with believability; I just assumed everyone would believe me. However, Monsignor Clark was polite and very professional. He tried to be as helpful as possible, but I felt that without the backing of the other two girls, he couldn't do much. But he reassured me otherwise.

There were a few times in Saint Agnes Church after Mass when I was lost in prayer and happened to see Monsignor Clark standing there at the side of the altar, watching me with a pensive look, studying me as if he weren't sure about me and trying to figure me out. Well, he had nothing to worry about, because I had told him the truth. There was another time when I was kneeling at the altar rail, and Monsignor Clark was giving Holy Communion. As he held the host toward me, he sort of hesitated. As I had my eyes closed, it seemed to take a while, although it was probably just a second or two. Finally, he distributed Holy Communion to me. Was he contemplating passing me by and proceeding to the next parishioner? If he had, this would have meant that he did not believe me, and that would have been too devastating for me to handle, because I take my faith very seriously, and it means everything to me.

In fact, it is the very essence of my life.

# Chapter 19

## Monsignor Clark Is Promoted

One night, around the middle of December 2000, just before Christmas, I had a dream about Monsignor Clark. I dreamed that I was in Saint Patrick's Cathedral, and the monsignor came walking briskly through the archway; he was dressed in the long black cassock with a raspberry-colored silk band wrapped around his waist, which symbolizes a higher status in the Catholic Church. Therefore, I knew from my dream that the monsignor would be transferred up to Saint Patrick's Cathedral. Even so, I was still surprised when it happened; I wrote to him and told him of my dream.

On February 3, 2001, he was assigned a new appointment as Rector of Saint Patrick's. I kept in touch with him through correspondence. I did not want to bother him because I knew that he would be very busy up there at Saint Patrick's, but at the same time, I had this unrelenting persistence from Our Lady, gently prodding me through little signals and signs, thoughts and visions when I drifted off to sleep, mental telepathy, and visions in my dreams. Spiritual activity in my apartment encouraged me not to give up, and sometimes I felt an urgent feeling to get things done for Our Lady or had an inner calling to go to the tree area. Perhaps I was too tenacious. It's like a driving force, encouraging me along, and somehow I have to get it done. So there was and still is a lot of praying going on, on my part.

I was also having impulses to go back to the tree, even late at night, where I had first encountered the divine visions. But I don't live near where the tree is; it is a good few miles from where I now live. It was not always easy to do, but nevertheless, I would always try to get there, regardless of the time or the weather, hoping Our Lady would come back again.

The last conversation I had with Monsignor Clark was at Saint Patrick's Cathedral in the summer of 2004. I respected the fact that he was very busy and that he made time in his schedule to see me. I showed him the photographs of the tree.

As he laid the photos on his desk, he exclaimed, "It's a magnificent tree; how old did you say it was?"

I answered, "It's about one hundred years old.
Apparently, priests had planted seeds into that spot of earth,
and through the years, it grew into this strong and
magnificent tree with beautiful flowers surrounding it.
Some of the locals said sometimes peaches grew on it, and
birds would always flock to the tree and sing merrily. But
sadly, now it's not flourishing at all because it has been
abused, and there are signs that someone is trying to cut
down this beautiful tree gradually so that no one will
notice."

I showed the monsignor a photo of a side view of
the tree and explained to him that about two years after I
had the divine encounter, I noticed a very large wound in
the tree and the sap running out of the center. I was stunned

and very sad; why would someone do this awful act to this beautiful and innocent tree? It seemed to me that someone was trying to cut it bit by bit to weaken it. I was totally devastated. This tree has been there for years, and it had always been safe up until now. I had heard that the new owner wanted to build a condominium there next to the tree. Would this beautiful tree become a victim to modern times?

A tree buries its roots in the earth, symbolic of a deep connection with the earth.

A tree lives on the earth, yet its branches reach up to Heaven. So the tree embodies a connection of Heaven and earth, of spiritual and physical realms.

Here, humans and the divine meet.

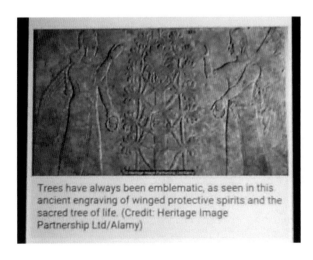

Trees have always been emblematic, as seen in this ancient engraving of winged protective spirits and the sacred tree of life. (Credit: Heritage Image Partnership Ltd/Alamy)

The Tree is sabotaged.

Notice concrete bricks stashed up against the tree.

I explained the condition of the tree to Monsignor Clark and told him there were signs that it was being sabotaged. Someone was trying to kill the tree.

"What if they cut the tree down altogether? She will not be able to come here." Monsignor Clark smiled and said, "Oh, Our Lady doesn't need the tree to come back." He then followed up with, "What is it you are trying to do, anyway?"

I answered him. "I am trying to do the right thing for T he Blessed Mother. The people have to know that she was here in this country, and somehow I have to do it, and I am not sure how."

Monsignor Clark walked over toward his other desk. Then he looked directly at me and said, "I believe Our Lady did come to see you. I believe she came to give you the message." Inwardly, I was thankful and appreciated that the priest believed me; that was a very important step first forward. Monsignor Clark lowered his head and spoke carefully and then said, "You have a mission."

He was right. I do have a mission—but what?

"Monsignor Clark, if only I could bring in these two girls to see you. It would be a big help to me."

Monsignor Clark went on. "You don't need those girls. Why don't you get the address of the owners of the property, and I will write to them, and we will get the ball rolling and get things moving."

One of the caretakers of Saint Agnes later told me that Monsignor Clark spent all night in the church praying.

I was ecstatic that he was going to help me and thanked the good priest for inspiring me to carry on with my spiritual mission. This is not an easy mission; from the very beginning, it has been very hard. As I have said before, I have had lots of setbacks. The devil is out there, and he and his minions are very busy roaming the world, constantly looking to devour souls and keep them from going to Heaven. Sometimes I feel like giving up, but then I think of Our Lady, the trouble she took to come here, and the condition of the world and where it is heading. Then I keep on going with this driving force, reminding myself that I am only the messenger, and a good messenger will indeed deliver the message, regardless of the time it may take. Heaven is constant and patient.

A few months went by, and I wrote to Monsignor Clark to inquire about his progress with the owners of the property concerning the tree. He wrote back to me and said that he did not have much feedback from them and that they were unhelpful and that I would have to turn to Our Lady for help (see Appendix A). I have learned that the Blessed Mother is very powerful, and when she wants something important to be done concerning the faith— saving souls, her Son's church, and the future of the world—then nothing and no one will stand in her way, not even the serpent himself, and not even the toughest rogue leaders of the world.

Yes, it might take a while, but the mission *will be accomplished.*

# Chapter 20

# Father Anthony

Monsignor Clark had been promoted up to Saint Patrick's Cathedral, and another priest, the Reverend Monsignor Anthony J. Dalla Villa, who had been in Saint Patrick's for twenty years, was sent down to Saint Agnes Roman Catholic Church on February 3, 2001. In other words, a switch was done. It was Father Anthony's first Sunday Mass at Saint Agnes. Sadly, he was met with some opposition from the parishioners, especially when the priest stood at the altar rail to give Holy Communion. This was a tense moment, because the parishioners felt the changes were too drastic. Standing to receive Holy Communion by hand instead of kneeling at the altar to receive it was just too much to ask the parishioners to accept.

There is something beautiful about kneeling at the altar rail, waiting to receive Holy Communion. It's an act of humility, so intimate and fresh—just you and God and nothing in between. The new priest just stood there, holding the little gold platter containing the communion wafers. I went forward and knelt to receive Holy Communion from the good priest, and only then did a few parishioners follow.

The parishioners felt this new priest was sent to make changes to Saint Agnes Church; one of these changes was to discourage kneeling at the altar rail to receive Holy Communion. And I had to agree with the parishioners about this change. It was unnerving; for many years it had been traditional to kneel at the foot of the altar rail to receive Holy Communion and also to say the Our Father. Most of these parishioners traveled for miles, and especially with their children, to come to Saint Agnes for the Latin Mass. Kneeling at the altar rail was a major part of the Mass for them because very few churches offered this service.

After Mass, I went over to welcome the new priest. "Hello, Father Dalla Villa. My name is Nancy; I would like to welcome you to Saint Agnes. I trust you will be happy here in your new post." He seemed pleased that at least some parishioners were willing to give him a chance.

"Thank you for the welcome and the big smile. It's been a rough beginning."

It was obvious he was unhappy and that he was trying to make the best of it. He continued, "Oh, you're Scottish? Just call me Father Anthony; it will be easier for you to remember."

We had a chat for a few minutes, and it turned out we had both graduated from Iona College in New Rochelle. Now we had something in common. This seemed to cheer him up a bit.

A few months later, I met Father Anthony outside Saint Agnes Church and we had another chat. He looked so despondent.

I asked him, "Are you all right, Father? You are not happy here in this church, are you?"

He looked at me. "I am a priest; I go wherever they send me." Then he went on to tell me his family was Italian, and he was going home to Italy to visit them soon. He seemed cheerful talking about his family. Watching him as he crossed the street with his head down, I felt sorry for him and prayed for him to find some happiness in his new post here at Saint Agnes.

On February 8, 2002, I was talking to my friend on the now-obsolescent street phone, making arrangements about where we should meet, when I suddenly saw Father Anthony standing by a deli on Third Avenue. He seemed to be waiting for someone. At the time, I thought he looked a little strange, not his usual self. I turned to call his name, but he was gone before I had the chance.

Two days later, on February 10, I heard the news that Father Anthony had suffered an apparent heart attack while preaching a homily in the pulpit during the Sunday Mass he was offering at Saint Agnes. Father Kazimierz A. Kowalski, the parochial vicar and a wonderful priest, was summoned from the rectory to administer the last rites. Father Anthony was a gentle soul. He will always remain in my prayers.

It's ironic that Saint Patrick's played such a large part in each of these priests' destinies.

Monsignor Anthony's appointment at Saint Agnes lasted exactly one year and seven days. And Monsignor Clark's appointment lasted for four years and six months. Two amazing priests: one fell in death in a state of grace, and the other priest fell in supposedly disgrace, banished from the cathedral and sent to Rome. According to certain sources, Monsignor Clark was accused of being involved with his married secretary for a number of years, which caused a scandal. And according to church protocol, he had breached his vows, and the media did not let up for a second. Every day, Monsignor Clark was in the headlines, and it seemed to be in every newspaper and on every TV Channel. According to the media, the hierarchy asked Monsignor Clark to fire the secretary who had been working for him for twenty-five years. Monsignor Clark refused to fire her, so he resigned.

People were calling me on my phone and saying, "So what do you think of your wonderful priest now; not so great, is he?" It was like the devil's disciples were trying to antagonize me over poor Monsignor Clark. Of course I defended him. Everyone at Saint Agnes was devastated by the news. This could not be happening to this wonderful priest, Monsignor Clark. I had trusted him and taken him into my confidence. I was brought up to highly respect priests and treat them all with kindness. I still feel that he was the right priest for me at that time. I also feel this was a direct attack from the devil because the monsignor was trying to help Our Lady. I chose to believe that he would not have betrayed Our Lady, because he loved her. He was a priest and an excellent one. Sadly, Monsignor Eugene Clark passed away in a nursing home in April 2011. He will remain in my prayers.

"Pray for me, Monsignor Clark? At our last meeting up at Saint Patrick's, you once told me that I have a mission, and now I will have to carry out my mission without you, too."

*But it will be accomplished.*

The devil is running out of time, and he is determined to drag as many souls with him to Hell as he can! The big prize for the devil would be the priests—this priest in particular because he tried to help me with Our Lady. Monsignor Clark believed that Our Lady had come to this city. The devil knew that this was real, and he had to drag the priest down and humiliate him in the worst way possible, to the point where Monsignor Clark ended his last days not as an active and brilliant priest but as a man who was deeply disenchanted by the outcome, he still believed in the truth of the Church. In the eyes of God and Our Lady and everyone who knew him—from his family and friends and students to his parishioners—he was not *just a priest*. He was an *extraordinary priest* and one of the best.

## THOU ART A PRIEST FOREVER

"To live in the midst of the world without wishing its
pleasures; to be a member of each family, yet *belonging* to none;
to share all sufferings; to penetrate all secrets; to heal all
wounds; to go from men to God and offer Him their prayers; to
return from God to men to bring pardon and hope; to have a
heart of fire for charity and a heart of bronze for chastity; to
teach and to pardon, console and bless always—what a glorious
life! And it is yours, O Priest of Jesus Christ!"

- Lacordaire

# Chapter 21

# Saint Agnes and Saint Michael's

*The Church of Saint Agnes is one of Manhattan's oldest houses* of worship. It is one of the most traditional in design, befitting its conservative, pastoral, and political role. It is a Roman Catholic parish where the Latin Mass is celebrated. Saint Agnes Church was founded in 1873 to serve Irish laborers at Grand Central Depot. It is located on Forty-Third Street between Third and Lexington Avenues in Manhattan in New York City.

Saint Agnes Church is one of the few churches left in Manhattan where one can actually kneel at the rail in front of the altar to receive Holy Communion. As I have said before, people travel many miles to come here to this very special and unique church. It is close to Grand Central Station, which makes it easily accessible for commuters and for many who work in the area and love to pop into church during their lunch hour or before they go home. In 1992, the building was destroyed by fire. The Pastor Monsignor Eugene V. Clark vowed to rebuild it, and he kept his word. (This is one of the reasons I went to him for help when Monsignor Falishione, who is the Pastor of Saint Michael's Church, couldn't help me.)

Monsignor Clark was a man of his word, and that was a very important quality to me. When he was reassigned to Saint Patrick's Cathedral, even though he was very busy, he made time for me because he believed in the story about Our Lady coming to this city, and he really wanted to help.

I went back to Saint Michael's Church to try and find out about the history of the area. However, it's sad to say that Monsignor Feliciano, the Pastor of Saint Michael's Church, was unavailable to see me. Therefore, I was reduced to telling part of my very personal experience to a so-called receptionist. I felt dejected. How was I going to help Our Lady at this rate? Can one imagine that the Blessed Mother herself appeared not even a stone's throw away, just outside of their church where these religious people lived in a nice, comfortable environment within the church grounds? Nuns and priests had parked their cars just under the tree and complained that the branches of the tree that Our Lady had stood upon needed to be cut down because the branches were touching their parked cars.

Of course, it is possible that they did not know or did not believe that Our Lady appeared there, and that if they did believe, then they would have known better and wouldn't have dared utter a word against the tree. Instead, they would have been down on their knees on this sacred ground in thanksgiving, highly honored that God chose Saint Michael's Church and this area to give this important message and warning about the catastrophe coming to this city and the world. Our Lady also knew that the people would need her and Saint Michael's Church for comfort and consolation. Sadly, the church was only opened in the mornings. It's interesting that the bishop Consecrated the little chapel within Saint Michael's Church on February 20, 1993. If given the chance, this church could have done so much for the families suffering for their loved ones who had perished on September 11, 2001. I was devastated, because I had known something evil was coming to this city, but unfortunately, I could not do much on my own.

I tried my best to alert people, especially the clergy within the church. No one would listen. I decided to go to Lourdes, France, and do volunteer work with the sick and offer this service up for the city of New York.

It was 1996. My deep-seated anguish was almost unbearable because of what I had learned from my experience and my helpless feelings at not being able to do more to alert the city. I just wanted to recapture that divine night again—a glimpse of Heaven—and ask Our Lady for her help. This spot here is a very special place where Our Lady chose to come to earth to prepare the world for what was to come in the near future—the final battle. There is no power on this earth to match her magnetic and heavenly power: the *Numinous*, the *mysterium tremendum*. The nature of the Numinous connotes "awefulness" (the terror of God or the Other World) (Otto [publication 1923.]

"Be not afraid, only believe."     —Mark 5:36

*Be strong and courageous.*
*Do not be afraid; do not be discouraged,*
      *for the Lord your God*
*will be with you wherever you go.*     —Joshua 1: 9

This is the back entrance to Saint Michael's Church on West 33rd Street.

2- Ver. 21. Michael your prince: the guardian general of the Church of God.

    ....you will be hearing of wars and rumors of wars

    ---then there will be a great tribulation, such as has not occurred since the beginning of the world until now, nor ever shall. And unless those days had been cut short, no life would have been saved. - Jesus Christ, A. D. 33

In his book *From Abyssinian to Zion*, David Dunlap describes the interesting history of Saint Michael's Church, which was founded in 1857. From 1861 to 1868, it was built in the Gothic style on West Thirtieth Street. The church burned down in 1892. Two years later, Archbishop Michael Corrigan dedicated a new sanctuary on West Thirty-Second Street. Unfortunately, in less than a decade, this property was needed for the rail yard leading into the new Pennsylvania Station. Plans were filed by Napoleon Le Brun & Sons in 1905 for a series of church buildings at 414 West Thirty-Fourth Street (G13) to be constructed by the Pennsylvania, New York & Long Island Rail Road Company at a reported cost of $1 million (real money in those days). The railroad numbered every stone at Saint Michael's, took apart the church, and reassembled it at the new site in 1907. (Cite is from Abyssinian *to Zion: A Guide to Manhattan's Houses of Worship,* Author David W. Dunlap, p. 231.

In 1993, a little chapel was built and placed at the back of Saint Michael's in honor of Our Lady. That leads toward West Thirty-Third Street, almost a stone's throw away from where the Most Blessed Mother appeared. It is very painful for me to write about this, because so many people were killed on 9/11, and for me it all started at Saint Michael's with the divine message (from God), and Saint Michael's was the first church I contacted.

"And the angel said to them, Fear not: for, behold, I bring you good news of great joy, which shall be to all people."

—Luke 2:10

# Chapter 22

# Why Here?

*What did all this mean? Why did the Blessed Mother choose* that specific spot and in this area? What could be the reason for her appearing just off a busy New York City street, close to Saint Michael's Roman Catholic Church and at the back of the Cheyenne Diner? It did not make sense.

I have gone over this a million times in my mind, trying to find an answer, if that were at all possible. My finding any answers at all entailed some research. During my research, I discovered that this area was called Hell's Kitchen.

## In Earlier Times

Hell's Kitchen is the area between Thirty-Third and Fifty-Ninth Streets from Eighth Avenue to the Hudson River in the borough of Manhattan in New York City. In the seventeenth century when the Dutch first arrived in New York, they found an idyllic, pastoral area of freshwater streams and grassy meadows on what is now Midtown's West Side. They called the region *"Bloemendael,"* or "vale of flowers." Many decades later, in 1881, the Hudson River Railroad set up a station at the future site of Thirtieth Street and Tenth Avenue, bringing major change. Immigrants to America, mostly Irish (fleeing the Potato Famine) and German, soon flooded the area and went to work in the railroad yards. With the burgeoning of industry in New York at midcentury, they were the workers in West Side breweries, factories, slaughterhouses, brickyards, and on docks.

By the start of the Civil War, the population of Hell's Kitchen had soared to over 350,000, and that population was housed primarily in rows of tenements that were quickly built among the slaughterhouses and factories. Most residents walked to work. During the 1863 New York draft riots protesting the Conscription Act, there were three days of chaos in the streets of Hell's Kitchen. During the Civil War, a rich man could buy a substitute to serve in his place. The rioters ravaged the railway in this district. The neighborhood people joined in and suffered terrible losses, resulting in mass burials along Eleventh Avenue. The number of men killed in the riots might never be known, but estimates range from two thousand to twenty thousand.

Another eight thousand were wounded and there was $5 million in property damage.

The largest group of underprivileged families in the city was in the northern district of Hell's Kitchen, and they ranked first in pneumonia and cancer, second in tuberculosis, and third in infant mortality. Since the 1840s, the Irish have been the predominant group in Chelsea and Hell's Kitchen. The endless movement of freight trains through the neighborhood added hazards of congestion, noise, and dust to surroundings that were already grim, and Eleventh Avenue became known as Death Valley.

The history of this area explains the plight of these poor people who lived under horrendous and unbearable conditions of extreme poverty, filth, disease, and constant death. One can only imagine the desperate prayers and sacrifices offered up to Heaven, continuously imploring the sweet protection of Our Lady. It is now beginning to make sense to me—the unfolding of world events, the acceleration toward the end of time as we know it.

This is a satellite view of the Tree between
Cheyenne Diner and St. Michael's RC. Church.

New York City.

# Chapter 23

# The Miracle of the Rock

*The photo will show the history of the tree that has been around* for at least 150 years. It is not a coincidence that the area surrounding this tree is called "Image of the Rock." The Blessed Mother certainly knows what she is doing. I believe that she chose that specific place for her own reasons that only she knows.

*Shacks and tenements in Hell's Kitchen and Sebastopol (the Rock), ca 1890*

12

Hollow of the Rock

In 1858, Our Lady chose Massabielle in Lourdes to appear to Bernadette, a girl whose family was so poor that they lived in a *cachot* (French for "jailhouse") that was once used for prisoners. Apparently, it was too dingy even for the prisoners to live in, and so it was abandoned. On this day, there was no heat in the house, and there was almost no firewood left, except for the last few sticks. The last batch had been sold the night before to buy food. The family shivered from the cold and dampness, which only added to their misery.

Bernadette wanted to help and begged her mother to let her go and fetch some firewood with her sister Toinette and a friend, Jeanne Abadie. Bernadette's mother hesitated because she was afraid to let Bernadette go out in the cold, fearing that it might bring on an asthma attack. It was a depressing start to the day. The mist came down, mingling with the drizzling rain, and a dark and gloomy sky hung over this icy, cold January winter morning.

At that time in Massabielle, there were plenty of fields, meadows, hills, and freshwater streams. The girls had to cross the river and were now in the water, carrying the firewood from the other side of the river to take home, but they did not want Bernadette to come into the cold water because of her asthma. So Bernadette chose a spot to rest, and that spot just happened to be the area around an ancient tree. It is interesting that Bernadette chose that specific spot to rest a little while on a rock.

The land was very spacious. Bernadette could easily have chosen another part of the meadow that was much nearer to where the girls were at that time. Little did she know that Our Lady had also chosen that specific spot in Massabielle, which became known as "the Rock." I was unaware of this name and only discovered it very recently, having stumbled on this important information. Now, it makes more sense to me.

The area in Manhattan in New York City known as Hell's Kitchen was not unlike Massabielle in Lourdes, as it was also overcrowded and wrecked by infections and disease, coupled with extreme poverty and hardship. Death and dying were common there.

Another interesting factor is that in both parts of these countries, the people were indigent but very religious. For example, in Hell's Kitchen, the people who lived there were mostly Irish Catholic; the population of Lourdes was mostly Catholic.

In 1858, in Massabielle Lourdes, it was at the *gave* (French for "a swift-running river") where Bernadette sat near the rocky grotto that Our Lady chose to appear, a place most likely carved out of rock by nature.

In 1993 in Bloemendael (now Manhattan), Our Lady appeared again. This area had also once contained small caves and hills and was known as "the Rock, "Ca 1890) Image of the Rock."

Two different countries separated by six thousand miles and 145 years were linked by visitations from the Blessed Mother. They are both unique spots at opposite ends of the world and bore a message for the world. The message here in Manhattan was more intense, and to my mind, seemed more urgent.

I was in Lourdes in July 1996. I had just come back from Mass and was making my way up to my room when

Marion, one of the English volunteers, waved from the window of the hospitality room, calling my name to come in for a very welcome cup of tea. As we were chatting about Saint Bernadette and Lourdes, some French pilgrims came in to visit. Marion got up from her chair to welcome them and began getting the cups and biscuits from the cupboard while chatting with the pilgrims and explaining her role as a volunteer at Lourdes. To pass some time, I went over to check out some books in the bookcase. There was a little book that drew my attention, standing upright on its own on the shelf. It was an old book about Lourdes and the story of Saint Bernadette, where Our Lady had chosen to appear to her.

As I was flipping through the pages, I came across an old photograph of the grotto in 1855, as it was at the time of the apparitions. I couldn't help but notice the comparisons between the two sites, Lourdes and Manhattan: the character of "Both, sites, how they interlinked, and how they were locations for a beautiful and important message to be delivered from Heaven to the world. Though there is a century between them, there is also a definite connection between the story of Lourdes, known as the "Hollow of the Rock," and the story of

Manhattan, New York City, known as the "Image of the Rock." Is this a coincidence? No. I don't think so.

I think Our Lady picked out these sites for specific reasons. As I stated before, Massabielle, Lourdes and Manhattan, New York City in the 1800s had a lot in common. Both suffered from severe poverty and dilapidated conditions. In Massabielle, Lourdes, the local hospital discarded their filthy and infectious dressings and bandages in the surroundings near the cave, making this a very unpopular area that no one wanted to pass. In New York City, up until only recently (about 2005), there was a line of garbage bins that were used to discard food leftovers from the restaurants. The piece of land that housed the tree at the back of the restaurant was discarded and abused and neglected by the people who worked in the restaurants. They threw all kinds of garbage into the area; slabs of concrete were heaped up against this poor tree.

It was at this time in 1993 just before Christmas that Our Lady the Blessed Mother, accompanied by an angel, appeared at this site with a sincere message for America and the world. If you look at both of the photographs of the sites back in the 1850s even though there are thousands of miles between them, you can see both sites are similar; they are both depressing and unattractive and nothing out of the ordinary. And they both have trees: the small scrawny tree above the cave in Massabielle, and the little tree on West Thirty-Third Street in Manhattan.

The trees are also similar in that they were very young. It is also interesting to note that the distance between where Our Lady appeared in Lourdes at the edge of the cave and where Bernadette was standing on the ground was roughly about ten feet; it was the same distance between where Our Lady appeared in Manhattan to where Sheila and I were standing. From my own experience of that night, I found that it would be impossible to touch a heavenly vision, because there is always a healthy distance between the visionary and the vision that is occurring because they are in different dimensions; plus, we are contaminated, and the vision of Our Lady, coming directly from Heaven, is pure.

As for having an apparition of {Our Lady }every day and night for thirty-nine years as some people claimed to have, nothing of value has ever been added or said about these incidences. Moreover, it would be impossible for the human mind to comprehend, and you would not be able to survive and live a normal life in the physical world at the same time. From a true visionary's perspective, from someone who has had a real visitation from Heaven, especially from Our Lady the Mother of God, you are completely committed to the experience and it is imprinted in your brain. It is very difficult to carry on with a normal life, because after the experience of a vision from Heaven that is so animated, so magnetic, so beautiful, and so full of life, it lights and lifts up the soul. It clearly tells you that there is much more to life than we can ever imagine, because for most, this is the only life they know.

One cannot pin all hopes and dependence upon humanity and the flesh. "The spirit is indeed willing, but the flesh is weak" (Mt 26:41). A true vision is a true gift from God. The visionary, therefore, does have a duty to tell the story to help and show the way for humanity, because there is hope in the knowledge that we are definitely not alone in this world. There is a Heaven, and it is reachable as long as we comply with certain conditions. It is up to us where we end up, because we do have the free will from God to live our lives in this world any way we want to. Whether we make bad or good choices, each one of us paves the way for his or her destiny. Destiny, for us, is not here, but it is in the other world.

Our Lady told this to Saint Bernadette: "I cannot make you happy in this world, but only in the next." So we know there is another world. How do we get to that next world, which is called Heaven? With simple, sheer faith in a higher power, and above all, obedience to God coupled with hard work through faith, hope, and charity. Heaven does not come cheap, nor is it free! There is a price for everything in this world—and the next one, too. Obviously, this is not our true and final home here on earth; otherwise, we would be here much longer. And since we are only in this world for a short time, would it not be wise to abide by God's laws? The big picture is not here on earth, but out there in the heavens. Technically speaking, we are all spiritually homeless in this world.

However, there is hope. "Have courage, Heaven is your home!"


Our citizenship is in heaven. And we eagerly await a Savior from there, the Lord Jesus Christ, who by the power that enables him bring everything under his control, will transform our lowly bodies so that they will be like his glorious body.

--- Philippians 3: 20-21


We must see life in its true light. It is a dream between two eternities.

Time is but a mirage a dream; already, God sees us in glory; He rejoices in our everlasting bliss.

Heaven does exist- a Heaven peopled with those who cherish me.

St. Theresa of the Child Jesus

"Coincidence is God's way of performing a miracle anonymously."

"Do not conform yourselves to this age but be transformed by the renewal of your mind, that you may discern what is the will of God, what is good and pleasing and perfect."

Romans 1 2: 2

# Chapter 24

## My Sister May

*It was around the beginning of February 1994 when my nephew*
Andrew called me from Canada and told me that my sister
was back in the hospital, she was in a bad way, and she
might not make it through the night. Of course, I went to be
with her as soon as I could book a flight to Canada. So for
the next few days, I became my sister's nurse and
companion. She put her arms around me, crying and telling
me that she did not want to die. I hugged her and let her
pour her heart out. We said our last rosary together. I
stayed with my sister through the night and sat in a chair at
the end of her bed while she slept. During the day, I tried to
make her as comfortable and as happy as I could by
bringing her beautiful balloons and keeping an upbeat
disposition and reminiscing about our past in Scotland as a
family. And of course, we talked about our lives together
back home on Dale Street in Glasgow and about our faith,
in God, Jesus, and Our Lady.

My older sister was very devoted to Our Lady. She always expressed her concern about the condition of the world and said we needed to hang on to our faith through God, Jesus, and Our Lady: "It's all we've got." Of course, I would agree with her.

It seemed that I was only back in New York a few days when my nephew Stephen called from the hospital and told me the doctor said May would probably not make it through the night. She was so strong and so brave. She talked to me on the phone, and my heart was breaking because I was losing her. She was my only sister and my only witness to the vision of Jesus all those years ago. Suddenly, I felt so alone and was not sure how I would cope with losing her. I loved her so much. She was so beautiful.

My beloved sister May did not make it. She passed away on April 4, 1994. Of course, I went back to Canada to say good-bye to my only sister. As they were placing my sister in the ground, I searched the sky through my tears and broken heart, looking for my friend in the sky of many years ago; I didn't see him. It's possible He was there, invisible, where no one could see Him. But I am sure there was an angel waiting for May to take her home to Heaven. My dear sister May, please pray for me.

"Faith is to believe what you do not see; the reward for this faith is to see what you believe."

—Saint Augustine

# Chapter 25

## Bess and the Cheyenne Diner

*A few months later, I went over to see my friend Bess, who was* Spiro's sister; she worked for him at the Cheyenne Diner. (Spiro was the Greek owner of the Cheyenne Diner.) I wanted to touch base with her and see if she had heard anything more about the tree because she was the first person—aside from Father Falishione of Saint Michael's— I had told about what had happened at the tree, and she was the first person who went with me to see the tree because the tree was in the back garden that was more or less attached to the restaurant. She explained to me that they were Orthodox Christians, but she would talk to her brother Spiro anyway and tell him what had happened at the tree.

There was a back entrance to the restaurant that I sometimes used because that was where Bess usually worked. But that night, a waitress was working there instead of Bess. Then I noticed Spiro standing up at the front of the restaurant; he usually stands near the door by the cash register.

West 33<sup>rd</sup> Street 9<sup>th</sup>Avenue, notice the blue globe across
from the tree.

Walking toward him, I smiled and waved and said,
"Hi, Spiro, how is everything? I have come to see Bess. I
thought I saw her standing at the window, and I wanted to
speak to her. Is she here tonight?"

Spiro looked straight at me and said, "She's gone!"
He then turned sharply around and quickly walked back
down to the front of the restaurant, where he sat down at
the first booth, looking at the floor as though he were in
deep, serious thought. Beforehand, Bess had told me that
they were not getting along because the restaurant was not
doing so well financially. I thought they must have had an
argument, and she had just quit working with him at the

diner. This was not the same Spiro I knew because he was always so full of life and so good to the staff and customers. He was a family man and always a happy person.

The waitress came over to me, and I asked what had happened between Bess and Spiro. The next words she uttered hit me like a ton of bricks. "She's dead." What?! The waitress continued to tell me that my friend Bess was dead. She was on a bus in Queens, New York; she waved from the window of the bus to Angela, Spiro's wife, and blew her a kiss, calling out that she would come by later to see Maggie, her little niece.

That was the last time Angela saw Bess. Apparently she had fallen in the street and was rushed to the hospital, where she lay in a coma for three days with an aneurism in the brain. As the waitress was telling me this, my mind was reeling. Immediately, my thoughts turned to the tree. I couldn't explain it, but I felt this was possibly connected in some way to the tree and what had transpired there.

It was also strange that a couple of weeks before, Bess had told Angela that if anything happened to her (Bess), she wanted her savings to be to be placed in a safe-deposit box to be kept for Angela's children. Bess must have had a premonition; she was only thirty-one years old.

Because she was born in Greece, her family decided to take her body back home to be buried there in the island of Corfu. It was about a year later that Angela and I became friends, and I consider myself very fortunate indeed, because Angela and Spiro is an amazing couple and have a great family. Through the years, Spiro was very supportive of me and very protective regarding the visions of Our Lady and the tree. Although he did admit to me that a few years back he had once tried to kill the roots of the tree by throwing bleach on it because the rainstorms and heavy winds blew the branches and leaves onto the roof of the restaurant and clogged up the pipes. But after he learned Our Lady and the angel had appeared and stood upon the tree, he was a changed man. He even suggested that I should plant some flowers around the tree. Spiro also sent a letter to Monsignor Clark inviting him to come over for lunch and to see the tree, and a copy of the letter was also sent to Cardinal Egan. Spiro became one of Our Lady's staunchest protectors and her defender, guarding our knowledge of what had happened involving the tree. Spiro and Angela are Orthodox Christians, but after learning what had happened at the tree and near the area where their restaurant was, Spiro and Angela went through a spiritual transformation. They became more religious and sought another Church to learn more about the Bible to be closer to Jesus. They are now more involved in the church. This is a good sign from Heaven.

Spiro and Angela, Owners of the Cheyenne Diner.

Sadly, they had to close the Cheyenne Diner because business had dramatically fallen, especially after 9/11. I pleaded with them to hang on; I felt sure that God would help them. The owner of the Starlight Diner at the corner of Thirty-Fourth Street on Ninth Avenue wanted to buy the property from Spiro to build an apartment building.

At that time, the Cheyenne Diner was getting a lot of publicity because it was a famous restaurant; it was also one of the last old railroad types that were becoming almost obsolete. The Cheyenne Diner seemed to be constantly in the news, with the exception that the public was unaware of what had transpired at the miraculous tree behind the diner.

On the last day, when the Cheyenne Diner was closing for good, I met with the owner of the Starlight Diner and told him I was worried about the fate of the tree, and I asked him not to harm the tree, especially because he knew the story pertaining to the visitations from Heaven and the history of this magnificent tree.

"No, Nancy, I am not going to take the tree down; I will only trim around the roots and just trim the branches down a bit."

We walked outside the diner, and upon approaching the tree, I asked him, "Can you put that in writing, please?" His response was silence; he never answered me. I should have pressured him more on his plans. Having said that, there wasn't much I could do without the backing of the Catholic Church, and besides, I did not want to go over Our Lady's head, because I was really afraid to make a move in the wrong direction. And more so, I was also worried about offending God, who, I had learned from the message from the first vision, was very much offended by humankind already.

View of the Cheyenne Diner and the tree in winter on
411 9$^{th}$ Ave 33$^{rd}$ St.

View of the Cheyenne Diner and the tree in summer on
411 9$^{th}$ Ave 33$^{rd}$ St.

# Chapter 26

## The Tree Is Gone

*Around the middle of July 2011, I arranged to meet with Father* Richard Terga, also known to the parishioners as Father Richard, from my parish, Our Lady of Good Counsel. We arranged to meet on Thirty-Fourth Street and proceeded to walk to Saint Michael's Roman Catholic Church on West Thirty-Fourth Street between Ninth and Tenth Avenues. Father Richard knocked on the door of the rectory, and the pastor opened the door, but he was not in the least bit receptive to us. I'm not sure if he knew Father Richard was a priest. Father Richard did ask the pastor of Saint Michael's for permission to bless the tree. The pastor sort of nodded his head; I suppose that meant yes.

We walked back to Thirty-Third Street just off Ninth Avenue, where the tree was. Father Richard immediately got busy by giving the tree a good dousing of holy water, with ritual prayers to go along with the blessing. We then prayed together sincerely, and I took a couple of pictures of the tree, and Father Richard took one picture of me. I was so thankful and highly honored that Father Richard went on that long journey to bless this very special tree. He is such an amazing priest and very devoted to Our Lady.

*Trees are Sanctuaries,*
*whoever knows how to speak to them,*
*whoever knows how to listen to them,*
*can learn the truth they preach.*

JQR

This is the last photo taken of the tree- Blessed by Fr. Richard Terga.

Thinking about it on the way home, I remarked to Father Richard, "You did not have to ask for permission to bless the tree because the tree is not attached to Saint Michael's Church."

A couple of weeks later when I came back from Lourdes, my friend Jennifer had left a message on my phone.

"Hello, Nancy, it's Jennifer. I'm not sure if you are back from Lourdes yet, but I was on the bus, and as it passed by the Cheyenne Diner, on West Thirty-Third Street, I did not see the tree. I am so sorry to tell you that the tree is gone."

I was devastated; the thing that I had been dreading all along was that this magnificent tree would be cut down. This was my worst fear—that the tree would be destroyed.

The following day, I called the owner of the Starlight Diner and asked him what had happened and why he had taken the tree down. The tree was over one hundred years old and was of historical significance, and what's more, he promised me that he would not touch it. When I asked him again about the tree, he replied, "Yes, I took it down because it was deteriorating."

But what I found out later from another source was that he went over to the real estate office and asked for permission to take the tree down. The owner agreed, for a sum of money, so there was an exchange of money to get rid of this beautiful and blessed tree. Two months before that happened, I had contacted the City Parks Department, and they had suggested putting a guard around it for protection. But having said that, the park ranger also told me that because it was private property, there was not much I (or they) could do.

The owner of the Starlight Diner clearly did not have the tree's best interest at heart. The people in the neighborhood who loved and enjoyed the tree for years were clearly upset about the tree being chopped down without their knowledge until the last minute. Apparently, some of the neighbors were in tears and asked the tree cutter why he was taking the tree down. He did not answer; he just kept on chopping the branches down.

For years, I had passed by that tree four times a week and never took much notice of it—that is, until that unforgettable night when Our Lady and the angel appeared in and around the tree. After that, whenever I visited the tree, I was often exhilarated and filled with total happiness. Other times, I would visit the tree at night, and upon nearing the tree, I would feel a sense of trepidation, like a premonition that something dreadful was going to happen to this city and also to this magnificent tree. I was powerless to help, mainly because I was trying to protect the secret of Our Lady being there, and the tree, and also protect the identities of the other two women who were with me on that very special night because they were afraid to come forward. They knew that once we went public, our ordinary lives would be more or less over. There would be no peace; people would want to talk to us all the time, day and night, especially the faithful. I was trying to protect their identities and also their secret (that they had been there and actually participated in this divine experience). It was clear to me they wanted to hide what had happened to them. They were scared and probably did not know how to handle it.

On another visit to the area and the tree one summer afternoon before it was cut down, I was sitting on the little wall next to the tree, when suddenly a soft and gentle breeze carried all the little flowers around me, circling me—they had the sweetest fragrance. It was a delightfully beautiful experience and was heavenly. This sacred spot will always be my little piece of heaven.

It's amazing, because before my heavenly encounter with the Blessed Mother, I had lived here for many years on my own and sometimes was homesick for my family. But after the brutal attacks on 9/11 that had almost destroyed the city and taken the heart out of it, my family started coming over here—thousands of miles across the ocean—to visit me and of course to see this amazing city. They came all the way from Scotland—my brother, Jimmy; my sister-in-law, Anne; and my nephews, nieces, and cousins.

Of course, I took everyone over to see and to pray at the tree quietly, so as not to draw attention to us. I know that this was a gift from Our Lady, bringing my family over here to share in the story of her visitation here in this city. Wherever Our Lady has appeared and her apparitions have been acknowledged—as in Fatima, and Lourdes, and La Sallette—she occasionally gives a message to the visionary, instructing that individual to go and tell the bishop of that area. The bishop usually ends up delivering that message to the pope, who, in turn, after much prayer, will decide whether to read the message. The pope then makes a decision to reply to the message from Our Lady via the visionary messenger who first delivered it. Usually, there are processions that follow, and pilgrimages are made from other countries to that place, despite long distances of thousands of miles.

It's interesting that after 9/11, Ground Zero became known as hallowed ground, and millions of people have made the pilgrimage from all over the world and still do come in processions to that part of the city. But sadly, little do they know that there is another very special and important part of Manhattan that also has a spiritual past and deserves to be honored, too because it is blessed ground. At the very least, Saint Michael's Church should be opened throughout the day and made more accessible for parishioners.

> Who Himself bore our sins in His own
> body on the tree, that we, having died
> to sins, might live for righteousness---by
> whose stripes you were  healed.
>
> -1 Peter 2.24

The tree lit by the sun.

# Chapter 27

## A Prophetic Dream of Warning

*I had an appointment at the World Trade Center on the 108th* floor on the morning of September 11, 2001, at 9:00 a.m. with a manager named Ben. But I had forgotten that I had a class that morning, so I called him on Friday, September 7, to reschedule the appointment for another day. He said that was fine and that I should call him later to make a new appointment. I never did call him back. The closest I came to knowing what might happen to the city was in a dream I had not long before 9/11.

It was July 21, 2001, at 3:40 a.m. I awoke with a feeling of dread after having a very specific dream that I wrote down immediately and drew a rough sketch of the round badge I had seen in my dream on a piece of paper, while it was still fresh in my mind. I did not go back to bed. How could I? It was, in fact, a direct prophecy. I live in a very tall building that is generally known as a skyscraper. It consists of two buildings very close to one another: My windows are large and face the front of my building overlooking Third Avenue. I am on the twenty-third floor, and because it's a high floor, I have a clear view of the sky.

However, in this dream, a large plane that seemed to be ready for war was heading straight for my window. As it came closer, the plane dominated the whole window, and my focus seemed to be on or inside the cockpit, which had an all-white background and was eerily quiet. I could not see any passengers because the door to the cockpit was closed. And there was only one pilot who appeared to be in his late thirties or middle forties. He had blondish-gray hair with strands that were partly peeking out from under his aviator cap down toward his forehead. His face was turned very slightly to the left. He seemed to be detached from flying the plane, like he had no control. The pilot was wearing a sort of Russian or Slovak-styled hat edged with gray fur, and the collar of his jacket was also edged with gray fur. My attention was also drawn toward a round-shaped, white badge, with a sort of symbol that was on the right side of his jacket just below his collar. I tried to focus in on his badge, but I could not make out any name or writing on it except for two black fine lines, one going down and one across, almost like a cross at an angle. Then the plane crashed through my window and my house, and everything went pitch black, and the building collapsed and came down with the large plane.

I remember my last thoughts were of Bridget, a kindly Irish woman who was my neighbor, and a church friend who lived on another floor on the opposite side of the building. It was a very strange dream, indeed. It was like it came from another time, like it was either caught in a time warp, or it had come to warn us; it was a direct prophecy for what was coming. Later on that morning, the big, heavy painting that had been professionally installed a couple of years ago suddenly fell off the wall and crashed to the floor. I told Bridget about my dream the following day. Naturally, she was afraid.

I do get a little frustrated with my dreams sometimes because I do not always get the message fully. It bothers me because I want to help, but sometimes, I feel powerless.

# Chapter 28

## September 11, 2001

Photo of Twin Towers

*September 11, 2001, started off like any other morning—nothing* special—except that I was taking a test at the Borough Manhattan Community College. The time was approximately 8:40 a.m. on a Tuesday. I was sitting in the cafeteria on the third floor with a colleague. Just as we were going over our test, she proceeded to get up to leave and said, "Let's go."

I replied, "We still have a few minutes; let's keep reading." Suddenly, there was a tremendously loud but muffled bang followed by another loud bang.

The cashier looked over toward me and said, "What was that?"

Looking through the window, we could see one man standing on the terrace, holding his head and screaming, "Oh, no! No! Look, look!"

By this time we were on the terrace, I looked up in time to see the indent of a large wing of a plane that had crashed right into the World Trade Center, straight through the windows, at a steep angle. Tremendous bangs were followed by explosions, and then fire erupted instantaneously at a frightening speed.

The professor came up the stairs shouting for everyone to get out of the building; there would be no classes this morning. Some people went out and joined dozens of people who were running in all directions and screaming for help and mercy, pleading for their lives. Some people were thrown out of the buildings due to the explosions. Others were literally jumping out of the broken windows caused by the explosions. It was scary and heartbreaking to see people jumping out of windows. They had a horrific choice: whether to die where they stood and be engulfed in this monstrous fire of oil that was mixed with concrete, or jump from this building that was well over one thousand feet high. What courage these people had, because they knew they were going to die this way. In fact, those two choices were all they had. Others were hanging out of the windows, trying to get help by waving their white shirts. When the second plane hit the second tower, our school was checked, and everyone was evacuated from the college on to the back street. I had not fully comprehended the impact of this disaster until what was to follow.

I was heading toward the second building to volunteer my services (I am a nurse), but the police would not allow us to go any farther because of the dust clouds. As I was standing there, the first building suddenly came crashing straight down to the ground right in front of my eyes. I stood there and watched with a feeling of devastation and so much pain because I knew the building was full of people—helpless, poor souls unable to defend themselves. And in that split second, I knew they were all going to die, just before the building came down with a vengeance. Then the other building came down like an avalanche. We then literally had to run for our lives. The buildings seemed angry, instantly releasing thick clouds of white dust roaring after us like wounded lions, devouring everyone who crossed their paths, as if they were trapped in the jaws of death.

As I ran, I spotted an ambulance and jumped in to offer my assistance. There was an EMT who was clearly working very hard and doing a magnificent job by himself. Nevertheless, I offered my assistance.

"Can I do anything to help? I am a nurse."

The EMT handed me a pair of gloves, a stethoscope, and some paperwork. He thanked me and quickly gave me instructions, as there was no time to talk, telling me to take people's information down, take their vital signs, and to clean them up as best I could. I immediately started caring for the few casualties that came out from the World Trade Center, taking their vital signs, irrigating their eyes, cleaning them up, filling in forms, and trying to comfort them. The casualties were covered in layers of thick white dust; they were businessmen, and one was an elderly gentleman who worked as a concierge in one of the towers. His clothes were all torn to shreds, and he was in shock but ever so positive, in spite of what he had just gone through. They were amazing patients, very brave yet humble and polite in the midst of this chaotic and horrific war zone. Eventually, I was assigned by a company to Chelsea Piers Trauma Center to work and help out. Someone taped the back of my jacket with a sign stating that I was a nurse, because I was a volunteer nurse, and nurses were needed badly at that time.

I have nothing less than tremendous admiration for the people of New York City and all the good doctors and nurses who came from different parts of America and even Canada to help out. Some of the people drove all the way in trucks, buses, cars—whatever kind of transport they could get to come into this great city to offer their help in any way they could. It was very inspirational to see all the people pull together to work hard and help the city in her darkest hour. The way the medical teams worked together and organized a large makeshift hospital, literally out of nothing—sheer brilliance. For example, they had color-coded rooms, depending on the severity of the casualties' injuries. There were hundreds of IVs primed and hanging from beams in the ceiling. Bandages were made out of sheets, all neatly folded, and tables were set up as emergency surgical beds.

*on my Way to Ground Zero  9/11/2001*

On my way to Ground Zero, 9/11/2001.

Photo: taken by first responder

The doctors and nurses were standing at their posts,
dutifully waiting for anyone who came through those
doors. Alas, they waited patiently throughout the night until
3:00 a.m. Only one little girl was brought in, stating to a
nurse that she could not find her mommy, and a brick had
fallen on her head. Sadly, I learned from another nurse that
the little girl did not make it. Later on that night, I was

assigned to Ground Zero with a team of doctors and nurses. I did not get the name of the good doctor I was working under. He was basically in charge of the medical team, and he had everything under control. The patrol police escorted us in a patrol boat to Ground Zero.

I was totally unprepared for what I saw. I was standing at the gates of Hell! It was total, raw, evil devastation. It was beyond my imagination. It was like going into a dimension of Hell on earth. My mind instantly flashed back to that winter's night in 1993 on West Thirty-Third Street between Ninth and Eleventh Avenues, and I wondered why God gave me that incident. I also wondered what lesson He wanted me to learn by placing me, as a volunteer nurse, in Manhattan on September 11, 2001.

At that time, it did not seem to make any sense, but suddenly it did now, standing there amid the ruins of what was only hours ago a bustling World Trade Center full of people busy with their lives. Now they were all gone; it now made a lot of sense. I had indeed seen the angel of the Apocalypse that night.

As I have mentioned previously, I knew that we were in terrible trouble, but standing here, I knew it was all connected. This was part of the message from Our Lady and the angel. The horrifying finality of evil from the devil, working through the weakness of humankind, turned this beautiful part of the city into a horrifying war zone.

I had a very sad feeling, knowing all those poor souls were deeply buried under tons of rubble. I tried to keep myself busy by volunteering in any way that I could. At Ground Zero, there was plenty of work to be done, and that included eye irrigations and helping the Doctors and Nurses with IVs to be primed —things I had been trained to do—and helping with taking care of the firefighters, construction workers, and search and recovery workers who worked tirelessly until they dropped from sheer exhaustion; they seemed to have superhuman strength.

Silent Heroes: Police arriving on Patrol Boat.

September 11, 2001

I am on my way to Ground Zero.

Heroic Construction and Rescue team in Ground Zero on
September 11, 2001.        Photo taken by first responder.

Heroic Firefighters at Ground Zero on September 11, 2001.

"Great crises produce great men and great deeds of courage."

—John F. Kennedy

Later on that night, some search and recovery men brought out two bodies on a stretcher from under the rubble of One World Trade Center. One was a young woman. The body bag loosened a bit, and her arm limply fell down on the side of the stretcher. I thought about the fine line that exists between life and death. It is hard to imagine what she must have gone through only hours ago; it must have been pure hell and pandemonium in those buildings. None of this felt real; it was all so strange, and yet at the same time, I felt a little better being near all these wonderful and brave people—the firefighters, the police officers, construction workers, doctors and nurses, and ordinary people—who on that morning of September 11 became extraordinary beings. The firefighters, EMTs, and police officers, all with their adrenaline running to the max and above, rushed into those buildings to save people with no thought for their own safety. Then there was Father Mychal Judge from Saint Francis Roman Catholic Church, who was killed while he was in the process of preparing to give last rites to a dying firefighter.

Chaplain, Father Mychal Judge

I know in those buildings there were many heroes that morning, and I am sure the angels from Heaven were busy on that day, escorting all those wonderful and courageous souls into Heaven. Their souls are now in God's hands, in the best of care, and no one can ever harm them again.

One woman who was working in search and recovery was crying. When I asked if she was all right, she

very sadly replied, "I found a baby's hand this morning."
She was sitting there in this nightmare war zone toying
with her food on a plastic plate placed on her lap, but she
was too upset to eat anything. She continued on, "I have a
child at home, and I can't get there because there is no
transport, so I am using my cell phone to keep in touch
with my family and to check in with them." I asked her to
pray with me, and we prayed together. Recently, I found
out that Mitch—who used to work as the concierge in the
building where I live in R Towers—was also an EMT, and
on that morning, he was working at the courthouse
downtown when he heard what had happened. It was just
like Mitch; he probably dropped everything and ran to the
World Trade Center to help. Mitch was in building One
World Trade Center doing his part; he was helping a
woman get out of the building when the towers collapsed
and he was killed instantly. Sweet Mitch—he was a good
guy. Every now and again we would have a chat, and Mitch
always had his Holy Bible on hand. He loved the Bible, and
he lived by it to every word. I can't believe he is gone. As
of the writing of this book, Mitch's remains have not been
found, but I recently heard that Mitch's ring was found, and
I know this will bring great comfort to his father.

Every day for the first few weeks after September 11, I had a very heavy-hearted feeling; eventually it began to lift a bit. When I reflect, I wonder why all those beautiful and innocent people, who were just trying to earn a living, had to die like that. It all seemed so pointless, all those young people with all their hopes, ambitions, and dreams had to end like this. Every time I see and hear a low-flying plane going over the city, it makes me nervous; I hope that it is not going to target another building.

How do I feel about September 11, 2001? Devastated, hurt, and sad for all the good people who gave and lost their lives. It took the heart out of me. For me, Ground Zero represents the very best of New York City. Yes, she will rise from the ashes, stronger than ever. September, 11 will live on as a day of infamy.

\*\*\*

I firmly believe that September 11, 2001, was the first part of the message about this city, America, and the rest of the world. I wonder why God placed me at that specific part of the city, and on that specific day, on September 11, now known to the world as 9/11. Perhaps I was supposed to be at this specific place at that precise moment in time to bear witness to what had just taken place at the World Trade Center. I had the prophetic dream a few weeks before 9/11 of a large, battle-ready plane crashing through my window. And in the dream, we all perished. It was symbolic of what was to come.

"I am at the gate. Whoever enters through (Me) will be saved, and will come in and go out and find pasture...I am the good shepherd; and I know my sheep and my sheep know Me."

Do not be "frightened or dismayed, for the Lord your God is with you wherever you go." —

Joshua 1:9

151

# Chapter 29

## The Souls from Ground Zero

*One sunny afternoon, I came home with groceries, and upon* entering my house, I distinctly heard this very soft and beautiful music that sounded like a million harps and choirs of angelic voices in harmony and perfect synchronization, so very far away and yet so near. The music seemed to come from the study room in the back. Intrigued, I quickly put my packages down on the table and went over to listen. It seemed to be coming from the area where a set of little chimes was hanging that I had bought at Christmastime.

I called my friend Marie and put my cell phone close to the chimes to let her hear them. "Listen to this; what do you think?" She suggested that there might be a draft coming from the window or the vent. "Good, logical thinking, Marie; hold on and I'll check." I checked the windows and the vent and convinced myself there were no drafts; I said into the phone, "Well, Marie, it couldn't be a draft because the chimes are not moving."

"Hmm, very puzzling and very interesting, indeed," Marie answered. To add to the mystery, the whole apartment was ablaze with intense sunshine. It was just heavenly.

It was some time later when I realized that I had possibly picked up some spiritual energy from some of the souls from Ground Zero, especially after I said my prayers at night for all souls. The first time it happened, I was sitting at my computer in the afternoon, when I distinctly heard a child's voice calling my name; it seemed to be close by. A while later, and over the course of the next few months, other people's voices began popping up. Some sounded young; some sounded like adult men and women; some sounded like they were in groups.

There were different voices; some I could distinguish, and others I could not. Of course, I did not see them in a physical sense, but I could hear them outside of my head. I prayed for all the souls that were in those buildings that fateful day. I included all the victims in my prayers every night. There was a lot of spiritual activity around me for a long time.

When I was at Ground Zero that night, many people were walking about carrying large photographs and Xeroxed copies of their loved ones, expressing their anguish, saying, "This is my sister; she was on the top floor; have you seen my sister?" Or, "Have you seen my fiancé?"…"My, brother?" "My sister…Have you seen her?"

I would sadly shake my head no. It was the same question voiced by so many that night; I could only give back the same, sad answer: "No, I am sorry. But I will keep looking, and I am praying for them." That night on September 11, there were many people wandering the streets just devastated and in shock and disbelief.

I still have a couple of Xeroxed copies of photographs that some family members had given me at different times throughout that first night at Ground Zero. I put the copies of their missing relatives in my bag, and to this day I still have them because I did not have the heart to throw them out. I have never forgotten all the souls who perished on that fateful morning, and I always remember them in my prayers.

God was mentioned constantly in those first few days, especially that first night. The words "God bless you" were passed from one person to another, and not in a casual way, but in a very sincere and gut-wrenching way, straight from the heart.

Throughout the years, I have gone back to Ground Zero many times alone and walked over to Saint Andrew's or Saint Peter's, where I can pray quietly for a time, because the churches all around this area are filled with an atmosphere of peacefulness and humility that seems to put everything of today back into perspective. In other words, it sobers you and instinctively puts you in your place and brings home the reality of what happened here at the World Trade Center. My experience and knowledge of what happened on that special night at that location on West Thirty-Third Street between Ninth and Eleventh Avenues was, in actuality, the first 9/11. It was the beginning of world events that would follow at rapid speed and is part of the message from God.

"Everyone who calls on the name of the Lord shall be saved."

—Romans 10:13

# Chapter 30

# More Messages from God

*Not long after the visions of Our Lady and the angel, I began to* get interior messages calling me back to the tree, and the tension was building up. Sometimes, I would get these messages in dreams at nighttime, and it was not easy for me to get over there to that area, especially late at night. Also, the area was very quiet and deserted at night because it was part residential and part industrial. But most of the time, I had a feeling of great urgency to go to the tree.

There are some private, mystical experiences that I have had with a much higher power from above that I prefer to keep private. I can only say that they were special messages from God. However, there are some things I can reveal that hopefully will be beneficial to some people.

# Chapter 31

## An Angel of Light

On Saturday morning, March 13, 2005, Our Lady of Good Counsel Roman Catholic Church held its first Latin Mass After Mass, my friend Marie and I went to the neighborhood coffee shop for lunch, and we chatted for a while, mainly about everyday things. The weather was good, and it was a nice day.

Later on that night, after lighting the candles in my house, I began to pray my rosary with the background music of the soundtrack from the movie *The Passion of the Christ*. At approximately 11:40 p.m., I was sitting on the sofa talking to my friend on the phone when I happened to look up at the ceiling and noticed a perfectly round light; it was quite big and almost directly above my head. At first, I thought it was a reflection from the car lights on the street, or even a reflection of a mirror. I checked the window— nothing there—and looked for a mirror; I could not find one. I went over to the light to have a better look. Standing under it, I could see a very intricate, gold-colored design around the edges inside the light. I was mesmerized by it. I stood back a little, and a thick, white cloud began to form and come out of the light.

At that point, I was not afraid, until it sort of left the ceiling and hung in midair; it began to glide gracefully across the room. That's when I became scared and called out to my friend Margaret, who was still hanging on at the other end of the speakerphone. But I panicked, scared myself, and also disrupted this beautiful vision of light. Suddenly, it began to flutter like a dove and glide over toward the hallway, as if it were looking for a place to go because its plan had been disrupted. I could feel my heart move because I was very scared. Margaret had to hang up the phone because her dog was barking for her attention. I plucked up my courage and went over to the light, which was by now inside a shadow at the top of the wall closet. I noticed that the light had broken up into four small round lights, and they were all pulsating; perhaps the light or lights were just as scared as I was. I sprinkled some drops of holy water over them, telling the light that I was sorry to disrupt it, but I was scared. I believe that if I had stayed in that spot in the house, it would have manifested into a full angel to give me a message.

It's strange because I usually have the television on, but on this night, everything was nice and quiet, and all the lights were on, plus the halogen lamp, which was very bright. But this mysterious light was much brighter than the halogen lamp. Also, this mysterious, bright light did not fly toward the window or the halogen lamp. Instead, it went toward the hallway door, where it stayed. It was really very gentle, but I was still afraid. It was definitely supernatural. In fact, I know it was an angel because it was extremely white and very beautiful and timid and harmless—yet at the same time very powerful. It's just that I scared myself because it was in such close proximity. This was different from the vision of Our Lady at the tree because that was outside and there were two witnesses with me that night, but this time I was alone in my house—that is, at least I thought I was alone, until Heaven sent a messenger in the form of an angel. This beautiful and very mysterious angelic light could have been in the house for a while before I noticed it above me.

A few weeks after my first supernatural experience at home, I experienced more activity that became more intense. It actually began one afternoon. I came home, and after a while, I went over to the large window by the daybed to straighten up the cover, and I sensed a very strong presence over toward the kitchen. Was this an angel that had come to pay me a visit? It definitely knew me. The atmosphere was thick; I could actually reach out and touch the energy….But of course I didn't.

A couple of weeks later, the dreams started. One night, I drifted off to sleep at about 1:00 a.m. suddenly; I awoke to a tremendous crash followed by the door of the little study room slamming closed with a vengeance. At the same time, it must have hit against the set of chimes, which started to ring. I was petrified and so tired. I looked at the clock, and it said 4:20 a.m. I dressed very quickly and ran out the door and downstairs past the concierge.

As I hurried passed, the doorman remarked, "You look like you have seen a ghost."

I ran to the corner deli; the owner of the deli was very kind. I explained to him that I couldn't stay in my house because there was something there, and I remarked that it was 4:20 a.m.

He glanced at the clock on the wall and replied, "No, it isn't; it's 1:30 a.m." (The electronic energy in the apartment had somehow affected the time.)

He gave me a chair to sit on and let me stay in the store until morning. I was so grateful. I wouldn't go back up there to the house on my own, and one of the doormen came upstairs with me when I finally returned. I peeked in briefly behind the door of the little room and saw chaos. I plucked up the courage to go into the room, and I could see that on the top shelf where there had been two large white plastic boxes, one of the boxes had fallen off and landed on a small cabinet, which in turn had slammed with such force against the door. Those boxes had been solidly up on that shelf for years. It certainly got my attention, and it really scared me.

However, that was not the end of it; more would follow. A couple of nights later, I was in the bathroom fixing my hair, when suddenly the light started blinking on and off unusually fast – (electrical acting odd). The following morning, I was in the hallway, and this light again started flickering on and off quickly. I looked up toward the light and actually spoke to it and explained that I had to leave because I had to go to work. It was obvious to me that someone (or something) was trying to get my attention, and I know it was a spirit from another dimension. Angels are of high intelligence. (I had lived in this house for fifteen years, and nothing like this had ever happened before.)

About two nights later, still afraid, I was trying to sleep, when suddenly I heard a man's voice that seemed to be very close—practically near or inside my right ear—call my name in a very soft and gentle way, almost a whisper. It had no accent. Then on another night, I was asleep when someone gently touched my shoulder. I think the angels wanted me to go over to the tree, but this is New York City, and as I have said before, that area is hard to get to from where I live, and besides, it is not safe to be traveling alone at that time of night to a rather deserted area.

After that night, there was lots of activity during the day and also in my dreams. One morning, I was awakened by a chorus of angelic voices praying softly above me.

This did not scare me; in fact, it gave me comfort, knowing that I was in the presence of the holy angels and that they were praying quietly above me.

"Hush my dear, lie still and slumber, Holy angels guards thy bed. Heavenly blessings without number gently fall upon thy head."

—Isaac Watts

In the Scriptures:
Without vision people; will perish.

# Chapter 32

## The "Survivor Tree"

*On the night of September 11, 2001, after working all day at* Ground Zero, I was walking through the little park with a couple of nursing friends toward the boat slip where the police patrol boats were docked. One of the boats was taking the medical staff home. It was strange; everything was covered in this white, powder-like dust. The park seats were damaged and were also covered in white dust. It was so eerily quiet, and yet there was a sense of deep sadness, dignity, bravery, and sacredness.

It seemed that everything in the area was destroyed, except for a tree that was discovered in the rubble of Ground Zero following the terrorist attacks.

The tree was badly damaged beyond repair. However, it was moved to a tree nursery and eventually nursed back to health, and new, smooth limbs began to grow from its gnarled stumps. The tree now stands at the 9/11 Memorial as a living reminder as a living reminder of our shared strength in the face of tragedy. This Callery pear tree is now known as the "Survivor Tree."

However, there is another important tree mentioned in chapter 35, I would like to elaborate on, that was chosen by Our Lady, and the angel warrior who stood upon it to give a message from God to this country and the world. This was a magnificent tree that stood about one hundred feet in height, its enormous branches reached out onto the sidewalk; one could see this tree from a great distance.

These two very special trees were separated by no more than five miles, but they are clearly connected for a very special purpose in God's plan. Both of these trees were badly damaged, but for different reasons. The Tree on West 33rd Street had been neglected and abused by the workers in the restaurants. For example, they would pile slabs of concrete on top of this poor tree, throw garbage near it, and park their mangled delivery bikes at the tree. It was heartbreaking to see how this magnificent tree that was once so strong and majestic was being destroyed by man. I wish I could have done more to save that tree. However, God does work in mysterious ways. This "Blessed Tree" at the back of the Cheyenne Diner was so big and strong; it had to be, because this tree had a very special assignment. It would hold the very powerful and supernatural visitors from Heaven—the Queen of Heaven and the angel warrior. Both of these trees suffered severely. But they both played a very important role in the 9/11 tragedy. One tree died, and the other tree was resuscitated to live.

Whenever Our Lady appears in a country in the world—and I believe this is a first for her to come to Manhattan, New York City, in America—there are always pilgrimages made by the faithful to pay homage to the place where Our Lady has appeared. Sadly, no one comes to this area to pray there in thanks; however, no one knew that Our Lady was here in this city. And in this case, she did not even have to ask for a church to be built because luckily there was already a church there—Saint Michael's. This church was specifically chosen by God along with the Tree. (My sister-in-law, Anne, thinking logically, said that the tree had served its purpose. I had never thought about it like that, but perhaps she had a point.)

The Survivor Tree

9/11 MEMORIAL

This week I will be the gardener rather than the owner. I will cultivate the fig tree so that it becomes a Tree of Life, sprouting leaves of peace and unity, communion and community, reconciliation and harmony. This week I will cultivate the growth of these virtues in my heart.

*(Church of St. Frances of Assisi)*     NYC

# Chapter 33

# Hell is Real

*It was about a couple of years after 9/11. One night—actually, it* was about 3:30 am, - I was abruptly awakened by what seemed like a multitudinous cacophony of voices screaming from the bowels of hell. I was petrified; my heart was beating so, so fast that I clutched at my chest. The screams were getting furiously louder and closer. These voices of the dammed were enraged; these were the wails of hopeless, trapped, doomed, tortured souls with no escape from it, it was their prison. For a split second, I had the impression I was within the bowels of Hell itself.

This is by far the most frightening experience I have ever had, except for the divine night when the angel came with a message for the world, and when Our Lady was going to open up the ground and show me something, and that's when Roslyn called out. Perhaps Our Lady was going to show us Hell, as she did with the children of Fatima, possibly a reenactment to keep me focused on the message. Reflecting back to that night, it seemed to me these voices were in sheer misery; they were coming from the deep pits of Hell itself.

I did not go back to sleep- how could I? For the grace of God give me strength. Sister Lucia and her cousins were shown Hell, and because they were children, Our Lady stayed with them. However, I was alone when I was given this glimpse of Hell; I sensed I was near this prison of Hell with these desperate voices screaming nonstop. I want to help people' souls avoid this depressing and scary place by spreading this message to save us, God wants us to live a good life. We must pray, repent, sincerely; otherwise, many souls will perish! God allowed me to hear these tortured souls who are in the fires of Hell to remind me to pray sincerely to save poor souls from this damnation. Hell is another dimension that does indeed exist, and the lakes of fire are very real.

Once a soul unfortunately arrives in Hell, that's it; it is there for eternity-there is no escape. There is no chance of going back to rectify the life lived on earth. It's done; it's over. Hell is real and it is terrifying. It is reserved for those who reject God. Although I was taught about Hell through my teachers at Catholic school and the priests in the Catholic Church, and I believed in Hell growing up, I could never identify with the reality of it-but now I can. Hell is very real, and unfortunately it does exist and I do not want to go there, either. There is a Heaven, and there is a Hell. It's up to you, while you still have time, to influence where you will go at the end of your physical life. There is no turning back. Jesus spoke a lot about Hell in His teachings. There is no love in Hell.

***

The safest road to hell is the gradual one-the gentle slope, soft underfoot, without sudden turnings, without milestones, without signposts.

"There are no keys to Hell- the doors are open to all men." - Albanian proverb

*Hell has a way of reaching deep into humanity.*

"We are not alone on the journey or in the trials of life. We are accompanied and supported by the angels of God.....In consecrating Vatican City to St. Michael the archangel, I ask him to defend us from the evil one and banish him." (Pope Francis, July 5, 2013)

# Chapter 34

## Diabolical Disorientation

*At that time of our divine encounter with Our Lady and the* angelic angel, the visitors from Heaven, we were in peaceful times. Nothing major was happening in the world. All I had to worry about was taking courses and passing them. But soon those peaceful times in the world were about to change forever.

Looking back to that divine night it's interesting to note that there were usually cars, and taxis parked on the street. But on that night, there was not even one car or taxi, which tells me everything was prepared like that for Our Lady coming, so that there would be no distractions of any kind to get in the way of our divine encounter with the Heavenly Visitors. It was important to get the message out to the world.

All during the first vision of the angel as I have previously said, I was afraid because of the contents of the message that was conveyed to me by the angel. But when Our Lady actually manifested, I was not afraid. However, later on that same night when I was alone and it fully sank in—the whole impact of what I had seen and experienced a few hours earlier—I was really afraid. The divine power and the importance of the message from the Holy Angel and the Blessed Mother were clearly from God. For some reason, I was chosen to take the message, and in turn, deliver it to the proper destination, and that to me would mean going back to the archdiocese that had let me down in the beginning. Having said that, I can't say that I blame some members of the archdiocese; there have been so many reports of alleged apparitions that it is impossible to examine them all with the care that such claims justify. The awe-inspiring God who we claim to believe in and serve will from time to time break into this world and will send visions and apparitions to specifically warn and help humanity, but certainly not to entertain humanity. If and when Our Lady does come to this earth, it is usually for a very serious quest: the world is in serious trouble and existential danger.

However, years after this divine vision, the Catholic faith is still persecuted and attacked on all sides from all dimensions; the enemy is trying hard to weaken the strength of the faithful, but it only looks as if the enemy is winning at the moment. My duty was to deliver the message, and I intend to do just that through writing this book, because it's obvious to me that some of the diocese do not believe me in spite of delivering the message *before* what happened on September 11, 2001. Apparently, it takes years to investigate a divine encounter—especially one of this magnitude.

And yes, we are still in serious trouble and in very imminent danger, which seems to be escalating at a rapid pace. And of course, there is the danger of losing one's soul, especially for the people who are so lost. They live life with no spiritual safety net. The Blessed Mother also knew that the people would need her for comfort and consolation. God had chosen Saint Michael's Church as part of his divine plan, but sadly, Saint Michael's was only open in the mornings.

Since then, I have watched the world spiral into a diabolical disorientation, as was *foretold*; the world has become unrecognizable and will only continue to deteriorate. Diabolical forces have been unleashed in the world. Recovery of peace will be a gift from Heaven. Many people are suffering through wars in other parts of the world as well. Societies worldwide are also going through dramatic changes that are affecting families here in America and abroad. We are living on borrowed time. The question is how long and how far this "diabolical disorientation" will continue to spread.

It was on the morning of September 11, 2001, at approximately 8:40 a.m., two commercial planes were hijacked by fundamentalist Islamic terrorists of the al-Qaeda network and were flown straight into the twin towers at the World Trade Center, unmercifully killing thousands of people and instantly turning New York City into a war zone. The war had begun here in America and would soon quickly spread throughout the rest of the world. Since 9/11, we have had the war in Iraq, with thousands upon thousands of deaths in Iraq, and Iraq is at the moment burning; moreover, our soldiers are in the poppy fields of Afghanistan, struggling against drug smugglers.

There has been a dramatic rise in Islamic influence throughout the world, and the most radical elements include horrifically killing Christians (including babies), burning down Christian churches, and displacing many from their homes. China has emerged as a superpower, and not to forget - Russia, which is still a main protagonist in world events. Russia and the United States, both armed with nuclear weapons, are engaged in a growing conflict over events in Ukraine and Syria. At the time of publication of this book, Israel, who stands alone, is at war

173

with Hamas. African nations are also at war with one another. And ISIS is probably one of the most brutal factions the world has witnessed, drawing many countries to join forces to combat them. According to Sister Lucia, Russia was chosen by God to be the instrument to bring about the chastisement on the world. It is not for Iran or ISIS to bring on the chastisement. The world is about to ignite in flames. Russia and Iran are dividing up the Middle East which in turn will send more Refugees towards Europe, which is also being divided, including Canada, and Australia, causing havoc everywhere in the world.

Our Lady promised to Sister Lucia in Fatima that she would come back, and she kept her promise. She came back this time straight to the heart of power in New York City, America, just before Christmas in 1993. That divine night, God let me know that He was not happy with the direction of the world and was very displeased with the way people were living their lives. *We are in trouble down here.* I cannot emphasize it enough. When Our Lady came here to Manhattan, I believe it was to warn us of the dangers that lay ahead all over the world. She came to help us live good lives; to offer us hope; to pray with us and for us; and to stipulate we must repent, do penance and reparation, and resist temptation from the evil one. Our

Lady does stress that we must pray the rosary sincerely and consistently to bring peace to the world.

There is a controversy that in the past Our Lady at Fatima requested that Russia be consecrated to her immaculate heart in order to bring peace to the world. Many people claim the Consecration of Russia to the Immaculate Heart of Mary has been done, and others say it has not. Father Nicholas Gruner is a Canadian-born priest who was ordained in Frigento, Italy, in 1976. He holds a licentiate in sacred theology ("STL") from the pontifical University of Saint Thomas Aquinas in Rome (the Angelicum), which he received with high honors. He is a priest in good standing. In 1978, Father Gruner was given written permission by the bishop of Avellino, Italy, to reside in Canada after Father Gruner decided that he did not wish to pursue membership in the Franciscan community he had originally intended to join in Italy. Due to the language barrier, there was no real canonical mission for Father Gruner as a parish priest in Avellino. So, Father Gruner returned to Canada, where he became involved in his current apostolate. Between 1977 and 1978, a Catholic bishop of the Eastern Rite, who was honorary chairman of the National Committee for the National Pilgrim Virgin of Canada (NPV), contacted the directors of the NPV and urged them to place a Catholic priest on their board. Shortly after, in 1978, Father Gruner returned to Canada in fulfillment of the bishop's urging. He was placed on the board of the NPV and made the executive director. NPV has been given custody of a pilgrim virgin statue of Our Lady of Fatima that was blessed by Pope Paul VI at Fatima. Father Gruner was instrumental in bringing the statue into Canada and subsequently was involved in organizing pilgrimages. Under Father Gruner's stewardship, NPV has grown from a mere handful of people into the world's largest apostolate devoted to the propagation of the message of Fatima in its entirety.

Father Gruner (known as the "Fatima priest") is the president of the *Fatima Crusader Magazine*. Father Gruner founded this magazine, and it is published by the National Committee for the National Pilgrim Virgin of Canada. It is published in the United States with the cooperation of the servants of Jesus and Mary. The magazines are sent free of charge. Father Gruner, who has spent decades of his life promoting the message of Fatima, maintains that the consecration of Russia has indeed not been done, at least not properly. Through his many books, workshops, and speeches, he is still actively involved in his mission to spread the message of Fatima. According to Sister Lucia,

Our Lady of Fatima's own words concerning Russia are as follows: "Make it known to the Holy Father that I am still awaiting the Consecration of Russia. Without that Consecration, Russia cannot convert, nor will the world have peace…Only I can help you."

(To be said at the end of each Mystery of the Rosary)
"O my Jesus, forgive us our sins; save us from the fires of Hell; Lead all souls to Heaven, especially those most in need

***

If the consecration had indeed been done "exactly as Our Lady requested", all I can say is take a look at the world today: it is spiraling downward on an uncontrollable roller coaster into complete darkness that no human on earth can stop. Our Lady promised us that only she can help because she has been entrusted by God to bring peace to the world by interceding to her Son Jesus Christ.

Be strong and courageous. Do not be afraid or terrified because of them, for the Lord your God goes with you; he will never leave you nor forsake you.

- Deuteronomy

Father Andrew Apostoli, CFR, a founding member of the Franciscan Friars of the Renewal, has been teaching and preaching at retreats and parish missions for several decades. He is considered one of the world's foremost experts on the apparitions at Fatima. In Father Apostoli,'s book, *Fatima for Today*, he poses explanations ("The Controversy over the Consecration") through objections and responses to assure many people who are confused and disturbed by things they hear and read. He notes that Pope John Paul did indeed consecrate Russia to the Immaculate Heart of Mary. Sister Lucia herself supposedly said that in 1984 the consecration of Russia was indeed done and accepted by Heaven.

Almost a decade later, Our Lady came to New York City. I firmly believe what I saw and experienced on that divine night. Our Lady came here for a very specific and valid reason. And it is possible that she is still awaiting the consecration of Russia from the Pope and bishops throughout the world. I believe the main reason why Our Lady the Blessed Mother came to this city in America is because it is the epicenter of the world. America is the leader of the free world. There still may be time for the world to be saved, and just to be on the safe side, what harm would there be for Pope Francis to re-consecrate Russia to Our Lady's immaculate heart?

At this moment, there is an invisible raging battle going on for souls. The evil one never sleeps and is doing a really good job with help from his zillions of assistants, the fallen angels. This is his moment in time. But there is another time coming—a new time that will change everything. Christ's words in the book of Revelation were meant to echo through the ages and down to the end times as a happy reminder: "Look, I am coming soon; my reward is with me, to repay according to everyone's work. I am the Alpha and the Omega, the first and the last, the beginning and the end" (RV 22:12).

The world has undeniably changed since that night when Our Lady the Queen of Heaven came here to Earth to gracefully alert us of what was coming to the world in the near future. This may possibly be the last message from God for mankind in this 21st Century. God has expressed his great displeasure through His messenger angel that He is not happy in the direction the world's humanity is heading.

Luke 19:10 say's that "The Son of Man came to seek and to save the lost."

My goal is to continue in my mission to guide lost souls toward eternity with God.

I want to stress that The Blessed Mother is our friend and wishes to help us. She is all- loving and all- powerful in this world. One thing I did learn about the Blessed Mother is that she is very loyal, and really is our friend.

We are unequivocally not alone in this world; we have many friends and family above us in heaven. And yes, there is a "God," and He does exist; He is surely alive, and He is in control.

God will have the last Word.

*For those*
*Who believe in God, no*
*Explanation is necessary.*
*For those who do not*
*believe in God, no*
*explanation is*
*possible.*

# Chapter 35

## Without Sheila and Roslyn— Now Only Me

I have not seen or heard from Sheila or Roslyn for years (the girls who were with me on that sacred night when we had the divine visions). I did try to keep in touch with Sheila through correspondence. I sent her a Christmas card every year because I did not want her to forget what happened that night. It was and is even more important today. Our Lady, the Blessed Mother, said she would come back, and she kept her word. Sheila did remark to me that she felt that if Roslyn had not called out to us at that precise moment, the Blessed Mother was going to give us our instructions. However, I was getting the message or part of the message that night and even later, as I have related in earlier chapters.

During that summer after we encountered the divine visions, I was taking a class with Dr. Casey at Iona College on East Fifty-First Street on First Avenue. He called me over to tell me that Sheila had phoned him at his house, and he mentioned to Sheila that I had told him what had happened that sacred night. Dr. Casey proceeded to ask Sheila a couple of questions, and then he said that I, Nancy, needed the date when this occurred, and had asked her for it; he asked that if she had it in her diary or remembered it, to please pass it on to me.

Sheila claimed not to have the date and that she did not remember it, but then she told Dr. Casey, "Everything that Nancy has told you is true." But she made it clear that she was trying to distance herself from the incident simply because she could not handle it. She was afraid. Her family, not fully understanding what she was trying to tell them, told her to try and forget about it.

I do pray for these two women; at the same time, I wonder why God placed me with these two as witnesses: what help can these two be to me? I was conflicted about protecting them, the tree, and the secret of Our Lady's appearance. Talk about keeping secrets! I think this was the biggest secret for me to keep in this city, which in itself is a miracle, as nothing is secretive here.

One afternoon, Sheila and I were in the Cheyenne Diner. As we were leaving, we went to look at the tree, and she remarked about how there might have been a magnetic field around the tree on that sacred night. Evidently, she had been talking about it to people, but sadly, not to the archdiocese, which was what we were supposed to do. It would have been more beneficial to the people in the world if we had both gone to the archdiocese together and told the truth of exactly what had happened that night. I was sure that after the city was attacked on September 11, 2001, Sheila at least would get in touch with me—but nothing.

Even though I have been in touch with the supernatural through the angels and my vision of Jesus when I was a child and was the only one who could see them except for that sacred night when God allowed my friends to share in this extraordinary event direct from heaven. I never asked for more from Sheila and Rosalyn, but I am disappointed in both of them. At the same time, I feel it is important to point out that this is the first time Our Lady has come to a large metropolitan city, especially one like New York. Our Lady has always appeared in remote parts of the world to children of the same culture. And this is the first time Our Lady has appeared to three adults of different ethnic backgrounds. There were three different cultures there that night: Rosalyn is part Greek and part Puerto Rican; Sheila is African American; and I have a Scottish, and Irish background. Both of them had been born in America, but I was born in Scotland. I am an American citizen, but I could just as easily go back to Scotland and leave America, and if possible, forget all this ever happened. As for choosing the place where She appeared and choosing to appear to three different cultures…Well, perhaps Our Lady likes "cultural diversity."

Yet, I do feel that world culture will play a big part in the near future by shaping the new world order to change the dynamics of the world through cultures from war torn. Poor countries will be used, and exploited by the elites to their advantageous gains through sheer greed to gain domination of the world.

I never asked for this, but it did happen, and I will stay here as long as Our Lady needs me to. Why would I bother even pursuing this endeavor for so long if it were not true? I have nothing to gain and everything to lose if it is all lies and fabrication. As my father was fond of saying, "No matter what happens in life, always tell the truth! The truth will always set you free." I grew up with that philosophy, and I still live by it. Do not stifle the Spirit. Saint Paul warns us not to "extinguish the Spirit" by despising the true prophets sent to the Church by the Holy

Ghost: "Extinguish not the Spirit. Despise not prophecies. But prove all things, and hold fast to that which is good" (1 Thes 19–21).

Thus, in my own way and in any way I can, I am holding fast to the truth of what happened that fateful day in December in 1993, and I hope this book in part will help me get this important message out to the world.
The time has come.

*"The truth is like a lion; you don't have to defend it.*
*Let it loose; it will defend itself."*
                    *- St. Augustine*

# *Acknowledgements*

Thanks to Create Space publishing for doing a wonderful job in supporting me in this endeavor and providing me with an excellent publishing team plus the support necessary to succeed. I would also like to acknowledge the editing team and production team for their great work making this book become a reality. I am grateful to the sales and marketing team for enthusiastically promoting this book and doing an amazing job of it.

A special thanks to my editor, Madalyn Stone, for your dedication, patience, and friendship, and outstanding editorial talents. Your abilities were crucial to this book.

Also a special thanks to my friend Sean Mahony in the early days of this project that has come to fruition through his professional insight, enthusiasm, and inspiration in working with me on this project.

Thanks to my dear friend Fr. Richard Terga for his spiritual friendship, and especially for blessing the tree. That is now known as the miraculous tree.

Thanks to Fr. Kazimierz A. Kowalski for encouraging me to me to use my talent, and write this book. Not forgetting my friends who kept encouraging me to go on especially when I felt like giving up.

Thank you, Monsignor Eugene Clark for believing in me and for your spiritual guidance pertaining to my faith, and Our Lady.

Lastly, a big thank you to my nephew Paul, for being sincerely helpful in keeping me going, with his wise advice and sending me many emails across the pond to enquire about the book.

Thanks to my wonderful sister-in-law Anne for her encouragement in listening, and feedback and pushing me along the way to continue on with this important book.

Thanks, to the Compucare Team for their professional expertise, in assisting me and sorting out any problems that arose with my computer.

Last, but not least, I wish to thank God, for giving me the Grace, and strength to finally finish this book.

# Appendix A

## Correspondence

6/5/96.

Dear Monsieur O'Donnell,

I thought, and prayed about this. I want you to have the original letter that you read last week. I have made a copy for myself. I also sent a copy to Monsieur Clark of St Agnes.

Thank you.

Yours Sincerely.

Agnes Nancy Mc Gill.

God Bless you.

Thank you for at least seeing me.

NYC NY 10128
9/27/02.

Dear Monsignor Clark,                    212 828 2138.

     In Reference to our meeting on September 18th 2002) I haven Inclosed the name, and address of the owner of the building that you requested conerening the tree:) I have also Inclosed the owner name, and address of the Restaurant, his name is Spiro Kasimmas, he will give you any additional information Should you require it also the exact location of the Tree:

     Thank you so much.

     Monsignor Clark)

     Yours humbly.

     Nancy McGill.

"I really appreciate your help,"

June 27, 2003

Cheyenne Diner
411 9th Avenue
New York, NY 10001
(212) 465-8750

Dear Monsignor Clark,

My name is Spiro Kasimis and I own the Cheyenne Diner on West 33rd Street. My friend Nancy McGill speaks very highly of you. I understand you had contacted the people involved with the 33rd street property, but they did not know about the Apparition connected to the Tree.

The Tree was planted by priests about 100 years ago. There is a beautiful history attached to it. Everything that Nancy has told you about the Apparition of our Lady is true - I can attest to this.

I spoke with the other girl, shiela and she told me that she did see a beautiful Lady in shimmering light, almost transparent, hovering upon the tree. Her hands folded in prayer, gazing straight ahead with her head tilted slightly upwards. All this happened before, September 11, 2001.

Personally, I feel it would be in the public's interest to know what happened here. It does not seem right to keep this hidden. If you have any questions, I would be more than willing to discuss the apparition of that night, and the events concerning the tree.

Sincerely,

S.K.

cc: To his Eminence Edward Cardinal Egan

190

# Cathedral of Saint Patrick

March 31, 2003

Dear Nancy:

Thank you for your letter of March 17th. Some long time ago, I wrote to the people involved and received a very unhelpful answer. I haven't heard anything since then.

You will have to turn to Our Lady for help.

Kindest wishes,

*E.o.Cul*

Monsignor Eugene V. Clark

EVC/ld

Ms. Nancy McGill

191

October 1, 2010

Dear Ms. McGill:

    Thank you most sincerely for your letter of September 14, 2010, together with the enclosed donation in the amount of fifty dollars ($50.00) to Saint Patrick's Cathedral. Your thoughtfulness and generosity are deeply appreciated.

    As to meeting with you, I would first ask that you meet with your pastor. He can then communicate with me, by telephone or letter, at which time we can determine how best to proceed. For matters such as the one that you have so kindly brought to my attention, this has been the praxis of the archdiocese, and I have chosen to follow it since my appointment as archbishop. I trust that you will understand.

    With prayerful best wishes, I am,

                Faithfully in Christ,

                Most Reverend Timothy M. Dolan
                Archbishop of New York

Subj:      **311 / Service Request #: C1-1-519464805 / Illegal Tree Damage**
Date:      10/29/09 9:41:22 AM Pacific Standard Time
From:      SRNotification@customerservice.nyc.gov
To:        NANMCGI@AOL.COM
*Sent from the Internet (Details)*

**This is an auto-generated system message. Please do not reply to this message.**

Service Request #: C1-1-519464805
Date Submitted: 10/29/09 1:35:50 PM

Your service request has been routed to the Department of Parks and Recreation for action.

To learn about the status of your request, please follow the link below to the 311 Service Request Look-Up page:

Service Request Look Up

Please note that it may take up to 24 hours for new Service Requests to be available on the Look-Up Page. Once a Service Request is updated, it may take up to 24 hours for the change to be reflected.

Thank you,

The 311 Customer Service Team

--------------------------------

For information about City services, visit NYC.gov.

For information about the 311 Privacy Policy, click on the link below:
http://www.nyc.gov/html/doitt/html/about/about_311.shtml

If any of the links in this email do not work, please copy and paste the link into your browser's address bar.

Thursday, October 29, 2009 America Online: NanMcgi

193

1619 3<sup>rd</sup> Ave apt 23E
N.Y.C.10128
February 17, 2011

Greetings Father Kowalski,

Here is the letter from Bishop Timothy Dolan.I would greatly appreciate it if you can call him or write as he requested. I understand you are very busy. I chose you because you are the Pastor of Our Lady of Good Counsel RC Church within my neighborhood. You know the background story about the Blessed Mother appearing to the three nurses outside of St. Michael's RC Church on west 33rd Street before September 11,2001. Since then, I have been trying to do the proper thing for Our Lady however, no one seems to care and I find that very sad.

Last year you seemed very interested in the story and you even asked me for a copy of the document. I know you have a lot to deal with in your own Church but I trust you will find time plus you will know what to do because you are such an efficient Priest. I feel that there is a great disservice being done to Our lady when {She} is pushed aside for the intricacies of the modern world. Although I am fully aware of the higher hierarchy being cautious and I totally agree with their mission statement and commitment on these very delicate matters concerning the True Faith. However this is real, it happened, and no one can ever take that away. At least, the Bishop should know and he is entitled to know what happened here in this city.

Sincerely,

Agnes N Mc Gill

Reference of a Hospitalier, Councillor, or "Responsable de Service" who knows the applicant well and is able to vouch for the quality of his service in Lourdes.

I have known Nancy McGee for 17 years. She is
an exceptional lady with a profound sense of
charity and concern for others; moreover, she is a very
knowledgeable and devout Catholic woman. She
has also a great sense of responsibility, and is
well qualified being that she is a nurse.

Recommendation of the Diocesan or National Hospitality to which the applicant belongs or alternatively from the President of a charitable organisation in his/her parish confirming his/her good character and actions.

Rev. Richard Joyce Suga, CICM
Associate Pastor of Our Lady of Good Counsel

Recommendation of "Accueil des Stagiaires".

Applicant's discussion with a councillor.

Avis favorable      02.08.2012

Search Mail
Today on AOL
New Mail   1895
Old Mail
Drafts
Sent
IMs
Spam (54)
Recently Deleted
Contacts
Calendar
My Folders

Search the Web        Search   Enhanced by

Reply      Forward      IM      Action      Delete      Spam

**REQUEST FOR IDENTIFICATION OF OFFICERS WHO ASSISTED YOU ON 9/11**

Inskip, Charlene to you and Jantzen, Harold · 4 days ago · More Details

Dear Nancy,

I received the pictures you sent and your request for the names of the officers who assisted you on 9/11. Unfortunately, they are not from the Suffolk County Pol
shoulder patch, my first impression would be they are with the New Jersey State Police. I wish you luck with your search.

If you would like the pictures back, please let us know and we will mail them back to you.

If there is anything else we can do, please feel free to contact me at 631-854-8380.

Harold Jantzen, Deputy Inspector
C.O., Suffolk County Police Marine Bureau

Basic Version  |  Accr

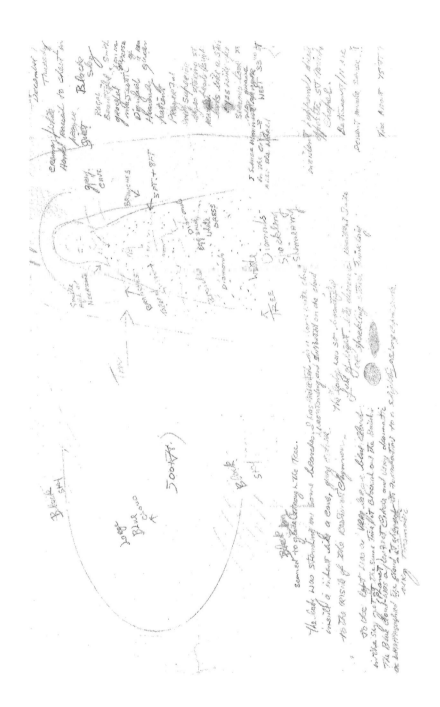

Time
( 3:40AM )

DREAM

The Pilot was about late 30s - (middle 40s)    (July 21st 2001)
Face hair, Face Turned slightly to the left.
He was wearing a sort of Russian or slovac kind of
hat. With a greyish hue on his Jacket Called Badge
with a symbol  O ⊕ .  The Plane was
Large, and War, or Battle ready.

198

The Grotto

FLOODS

SANCTUARY of OUR LADY of LOURDES

18$^{th}$ and 19$^{th}$ JUNE   2013

# The Blue Globe

"We both stood there in amazement as the planet-like globe began to loosen from the sky and descend toward the earth, coming down to meet us."

First encounter with the Heavenly Globe

Globe changes formation

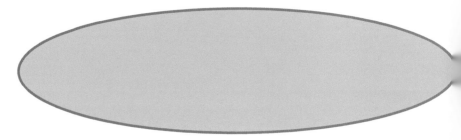

# APPENDIX   B

*The Lower Basilica near the Grotto, in Lourdes*

St. Pius X  Basilica Lourdes-France June 2003

Rosary Square

## Rosary Square Lourdes-France   2003

# The Hail
# Holy Queen

Hail, holy Queen,
mother of mercy;
hail, our life,
our sweetness, and our hope!
To you do we cry,
poor banished children of Eve;
to you do we send up our sighs,
mourning and weeping in this vale of tears.
Turn then, most gracious advocate,
your eyes of mercy towards us;
and after this our exile,
show to us
the blessed fruit of your womb, Jesus.
O clement,
O loving,
O sweet Virgin Mary.

*. Pray for us, O holy Mother of God.*
*R. That we may be made worthy*
*of the promise of Christ.*

202

# The Angelus

V. The Angel of the lord
declared to Mary:

R. And she conceived
of the Holy Spirit.

Hail Mary, ...

V. Behold the handmaid of the lord:

R. Be it done to me according to your word.

Hail Mary, ...

V. And the Word was made Flesh:

R. And dwelt among us. Hail mary, ...

V. Pray for us, O holy Mother of God.

R. That we may be made worthy
of the promises of Christ.

*Let us pray.*

*Pour forth, we beseech you, O Lord, your grace into*
*our hearts, that we, to whom the incarnation of Christ,*
*your Son, was made known by the message of angel,*
*may be brought by his passion and cross* ✠ *to the*
*glory of his resurrection, through the same Christ our Lord.*
*Amen.*

*Our Lady outside of Church in NYC*

*Notice the Blue Globe above the Bishops preparing for*
*the Procession, in Lourdes in June 18, 2003*

*Coworkers at the Sanctuary in Lourdes*

*June 16, 2003*

*Nancy at Lourdes*

# Firefighter's Prayer

When I am called to duty,
Wherever flames may rage,
Give me the strength to save a life
Whatever be its age.

Help me embrace a little child before it is too late,
or save an older person from the horror of that fate.
Enable me to be alert and hear the weakest shout,
And quickly and efficiently to put the fire out.
 I want to fill my calling and to give the best in me,
To guard my every neighbor and protect his property.

And if according to God's will
I must answer death's call,
Bless with your protecting hand,
my family one and all.
Perfect Pleasures

Fr. Nicholas Gruner, who died on April 29 2015, of a sudden heart attack, founded the Fatima Crusader magazine and was the strongest voice claiming that there was more to the message of Fatima than had been revealed.

RIP: Dear Father Nicholas.


Angel's Prayer

O Most holy Trinity, Father, Son and Holy Spirit, I adore You profoundly. I offer You the most precious Body, Blood, Soul and Divinity of Jesus, Christ, present in all the tabernacles of the world, in reparation for the outrages, sacrileges and indifference by which He is offended by the infinite merits of the Sacred Heart of Jesus and the Immaculate Heart of Mary, I beg the conversion of poor sinners.

Angel of Peace, Fall 1916

Apostles Creed

I believe in God, the Father almighty, Creator of heaven and earth, and in Jesus Christ, his only Son, our Lord, who was conceived by the Holy spirit, born of the Virgin Mary, suffered under Pontius Pilate, was crucified, died and was buried; he descended into hell; on the third day he rose again from the dead; he ascended into heaven, and is seated at the right hand of God the Father almighty; from there he will come to judge the living and the dead. I believe in the Holy Catholic Church, the communion of saints, the forgiveness of sins, the resurrection of the body, and life everlasting.    Amen.

*"And, you will see me coming with the clouds from Heaven. Sitting at the right hand of God."*

These are photos and Illustrations granted by permission.

Front cover photo of painting:   A Sign from Heaven

A Gemmail     Italian Artist

by Editor-in-Chief

Francois Vayne

Editors Dept of the

Lourdes Magazine

Lourdes-France


Lourdes

Floods 18th and 19th June 2013

Permission has been granted by

Sanctuaries  Notre-Dame

Lourdes

Fr. Horacio Britto


Rector of the Sanctuary of Our Lady of Lourdes

Photo Credits inside by Pierre Vincent

photographer in the Sanctuary.

Photo Credits: Lourdes-La Vierge de la Grotte

Cliché des- Monasteres de Bethleem –Notre Dame.

Du Saint Desert. F- 38380 St Laurent du Pont 508-

Reproduction interdite

Permission has been granted to use photos of
Cheyenne Diner, including the Tree and St. Michael's
Church. Michael Perlman Unlock the Vault

Permission has been granted to use Poster of the Angel
Never Forget - September 11, 2001
Artist Keith Hernandez   ART-AID

Photos of the Firefighters- the Construction and rescue
team Police on Patrol boat-were taken on September 11,
2001 at the World Trade Centre.
Copyright-Nancy A. Mc Gill

Photo: of Angel of the waters taken by one of the Doctor's
on the way to ground zero.

Photo: of Fr. Mychal Judge September 11, 2001 at the
world Trade Centre.
Credits: Reuters

Photos: of the tree St. Michael's Church
Copyright-. Nancy A. Mc Gill

Photo: Bishops in Lourdes on the grounds of the Sanctuary.
Copyright - Nancy A. Mc Gill

Photos: of ground zero World Trade Centre 9.11.2001
Copyright Nancy A. Mc Gill

Photo: of the Survivor Tree plus some notes taken from the book, The Survivor Tree with permission from the 911memorial.

Permission has been granted to use artwork: by Father Gordon J. MacRae. (These Stone Walls.Com)
St. Michael the Archangel-for back cover of book.

OUR LADY OF LOURDES

*Notice the Cross above St. Michael's Church.*

When the Heavenly Globe left the sky and slowly came down to meet us, because it was enormous, once it stationed itself in midair facing me, I could not see the buildings anymore because I was fully focused on this massive and beautiful planet-like globe.

The Miraculous Tree was on the opposite side of St.
Michael's wall where the encounter with the Blessed
Mother and the Holy Angels from heaven took place.

"Miracles do happen in contradiction to nature, but only in
contradiction to that which is known to us of nature."

- Saint Augustine

Sacred Area

# ABOUT THE AUTHOR

Nancy was always a happy child and came from a very traditional, working-class, close-knit, solid family of a religious, Scottish-Irish-Catholic background. Her extended family consisted of two older siblings (her brother, Jimmy, and her sister, Mary), her parents, her grandparents, and lots of aunts and uncles and cousins. She had an excellent grade-school education and was taught by strict Catholic nuns, "the best of teachers." Since her childhood days, Nancy has attended Mass faithfully every Sunday, weekdays, and on all the holidays.

Nancy came to America in September 1983 and settled in Manhattan, New York City, where she has lived ever since. She attended Iona College in New Rochelle and earned degrees in science and pastoral counseling. She also studied nursing in England and practiced nursing for many years.

Nancy also took a course over five years in the dynamics of Lourdes /France that involved the intricate life story of Bernadette, and how the miraculous waters in Lourdes came to be, which are now famous for its healing properties. Our Lady appeared to Bernadette who is now known throughout the world as St. Bernadette.

At the end of the course, Nancy was consecrated to Our Lady, the Blessed Mother, and received a medal for her service in caring for the sick at Lourdes.

Printed in Great Britain
by Amazon